Patternless Fashions

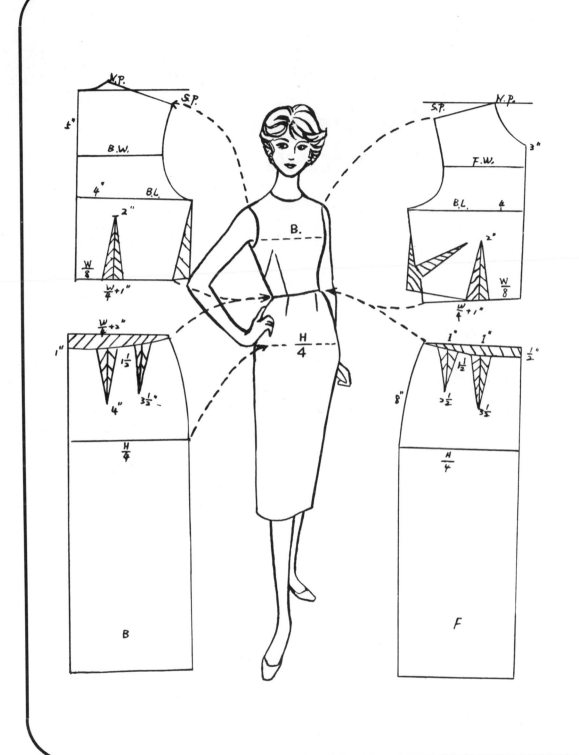

Patternless Fashions

Diehl Lewis & May Loh

How to Design and Make Your Own Fashions!

With New Appendices on Sewing for the Beginner!

ACROPOLIS BOOKS LTD.
Washington, D.C. 20009

ACROPOLIS BOOKS, LTD.
Colortone Building, 2400 17th St., N.W.
Washington, D.C. 20009

Printed in the United States of America by
COLORTONE PRESS, Creative Graphics Inc.
Washington, D.C. 20009

Library of Congress Cataloging in Publication Data

Lewis, Diehl.
  Patternless fashions.

  1. Costume design.   2.   Dressmaking.   I.   Loh, May,
joint author.   II.   Title.
TT507.L466   646.4'07   80-23125
ISBN 0-87491-416-7
ISBN 0-87491-413-2 (pbk.)

DEDICATED TO

My daughter Riggs

who patiently kept busy making her clothes without
patterns while mother wrote this book

Contents

Preface

I wrote this book because after living and studying in Taiwan for four years I had learned that there was a better way to design clothes than by using standard patterns.

From May Loh, my collaborator in writing this book, I learned the Oriental method of creating a dress from a picture—by taking exact measurements, marking them with chalk directly on the material, then cutting and sewing the clothes to completion. One great advantage of using this method is the elimination of major sewing expenses; namely, the standard paper pattern and the dress form.

The whole purpose of this classic technique is to teach how styles can be adapted or copied to present or past designs. The Chinese have for centuries used these few basic techniques to create any design that is fashionable. For these reasons this book can never be outdated.

Instructions are included for designing all types of clothing—from evening dresses to hot pants, men's bathrobes to children's sunsuits. Over eighty formulas illustrated in this book will permit the sewing enthusiast to design her own clothing and take advantage of changing styles. For example, by interchanging different formulas, a puff sleeve can be put on a "V" neck blouse. The varieties of creative combinations are countless.

MAKE-IT-YOURSELF PATTERNLESS FASHIONS is written to help the novice or professional make better fitting, more attractive, economical clothes. It shows how to obtain the perfect fit by designing clothes that conform exactly to personal measurements and accentuate your best features.

Diehl Lewis

Foreword

One of the most appealing aspects of making your own clothes is the freedom to design clothes that are uniquely your own. Along with this goes a certain responsibility to yourself to create looks that are flattering to you. There are certain rules of design that are as easy to follow as the rules of Patternless Fashions. With them, you can create a truly distinctive and attractive wardrobe.

1. COLOR

Color can shorten and it can lengthen, it can slim and it can broaden, it can attract and it can detract, it can hide and it can show you off.

Use a single color to create a longer look. An outfit that is all one color will make you look taller, as will one in monotones because one color makes the eye take in the whole figure in one sweep.

On the other hand, if you want to appear slightly shorter, then the object is to stop the eye halfway down, at the waist. You will, in effect, be cutting your figure in half. The stronger the contrast between top and bottom, the less tall you will look. A dress with a white top and black skirt, for example, will make you look shorter than one all in black.

In the same vein, the lighter and brighter the color, the broader the look. A woman who is too thin should lean towards white and strong brights. A woman who is on the heavier side should choose colors that are deeper and darker.

Prints, too, have an effect on the eye. The smaller the print the less it attracts the eye and the more it gives the illusion of a solid color. Bigger prints will make you look bigger. Patterns in dark tones will make you look thinner, while those in bright colors will do the opposite.

2. LINE

Line can also create illusion. Full sleeves, full bodices, and full skirts add roundness to the figure. If your arms are too thin, try wearing sleeves with softness to them. If you are smaller through the top than through the hips (most American women are), balance your figure by wearing slightly fuller tops. Blousing, shirring, pleating and tucking all add width to the bodice. Wear a skirt with a hint of slimness, such as a drindl or A-line, and you will achieve your most attractive look. If your hips are narrower than your bodice, then you can get balance with fuller skirts and slimmer blouse lines.

Lines that go up and down will make you look taller. A top with tucking at the shoulders or shoulder pads worn with a slim skirt or pant will lengthen your figure by raising the viewer's eye. If you are full through the stomach, try a pant that has some tucking or slight pleating at the waist. (In fact, this kind of pant is flattering to most people.)

Another tip for the heavier woman and for the pregnant woman: attract the eye to your face, not to your figure. Framing your face with soft bows, lace, ruffles and crystal pleating at the neckline will attract the eye to the face and away from the figure.

Color and line can play such tricks on the eye that it is best, if possible, to try on something similar to what you are planning to make — before you make it. What looks good on the hanger or in a picture, may not look good on you. As you try on your chosen style try to imagine it in a different color, with perhaps a slimmer skirt or fuller sleeves. When you make your own clothes, you have the freedom to make small change in design that can make an enormous difference in how something looks on you.

It is a great joy to make an outfit that is attractive and makes you look your very best. As a designer, I spent thousands of hours creating new styles and new looks. It was always ecxiting to see something new come into being. If you follow these simple design rules and Patternless Fashions, the same personal wardrobe success will be yours!

Janet Wallach

Designer and Author of
WORKING WARDROBE
(Acropolis Books, May 1981)

A Word to Beginners . . .

The technique described in this book is really a very simple one—even for the beginner. First, it involves the construction of front and back torsos using your 25 body measurements and nine basic formulas. These torsos are then used to make any fashion you may choose, simply by drawing the torsos on your fabric with tailors chalk and making the necessary style changes described in the book.

Look at the Personal Measurement Chart on page 17. Have a friend help you take your personal measurements according to the directions on pages 2 through 14. Fill in your measurements on the chart.

At the same time, work out the nine formulas listed on the chart. Fill in the answers. Then as you work through the book, just refer to these answers each time you run into one of the formulas in the instructions.

After you have filled in your measurement chart, you are ready to construct the front and back torsos which you will use for making all fashions. Some people find it easier to make their torsos out of cardboard the first time. They can then be traced right on the fabric each time you make something and the design changes then marked on the fabric. This eliminates the necessity for reconstructing the torsos every time you sew.

Have confidence in yourself and in your sewing! You know that by using this method, anything you make will fit you perfectly.

1

Measurements

Patternless Fashions

The first step in dressmaking before cutting the fabric is to draw an original torso on the material. To make this original torso, it is necessary to measure the body accurately. The formulas mentioned throughout this book are the same for every figure.

How to Take Measurements Accurately

The person to be measured should stand straight in a natural posture and the measurer should measure step-by-step with a tape measure. Start taking measurements from the front side of the body. In taking measurements, it is important to make note of such shapes as high waist, round or square shoulder, or one shoulder lower than the other. A string should be tied around the thinnest part of the torso which will usually be the waist circumference. The string should not be tied too high or too low, but right at the wastline.

Drawings on the following pages indicate the method of taking measurements.

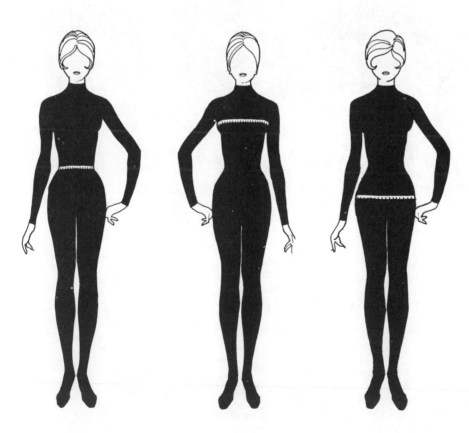

1. <u>Neck.</u> Measure around the front

    neck joint lightly, passing around

    the top of the most prominent verte

    bra at the base of the neck and i nner

    part of the collar bone at the front.

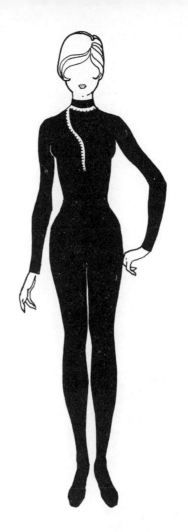

2. <u>Shoulder.</u> Measure across the

    back from shoulder to shoulder.

4

3. Front Width. From a position 3"
    below the neck joint, measure
    across the front from armhole
    to armhole.

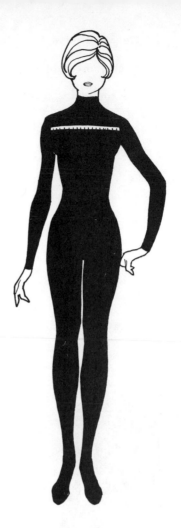

4. Back Width. From the most
    prominent vertebra at the base
    of the neck measure down 5".
    Then measure from armhole
    across back to opposite arm-
    hole.

5. <u>Bust Point.</u> The shoulder point is located
on the body where the neck joins the
shoulder. To measure the bust point,
measure from neck point to bust tip.
This measurement is not necessary for
drafting the original torso, but is useful
for designing.

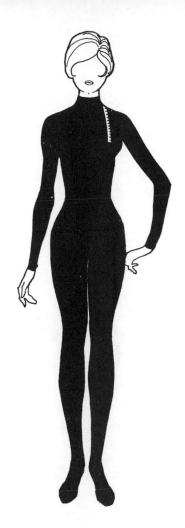

6. <u>Bust.</u> Measure around the fullest part
of the bust under the arms and across
the back shoulder blades loosely and
add 2". Do not use the brassiere
size for this measurement.

7. <u>Waist.</u> Measure the thinnest part of the torso horizontally and tightly.

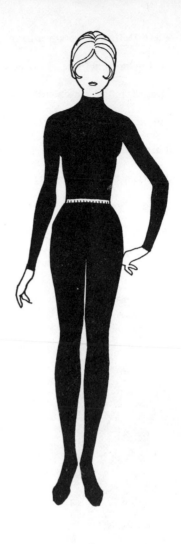

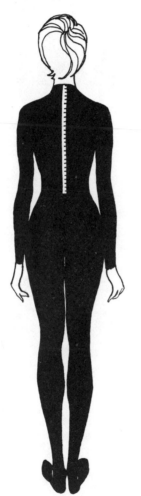

8. <u>Back Waist Length.</u> Measure from the most prominent vertebra at the base of the neck to the waist.

9. <u>Front Waist Length.</u> Measure from
neck point, measure over the bust
point and down to the waist.

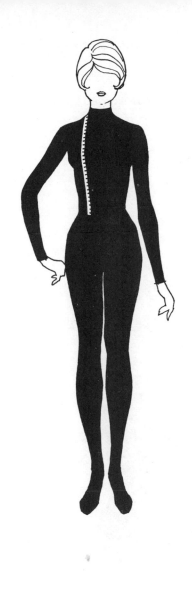

10. <u>Skirt Length</u>. Measure from the waist
down to the knee or desired length.

11. <u>Hip.</u> Eight inches down from the waist, measure loosely around the thickest part horizontally and add 1".

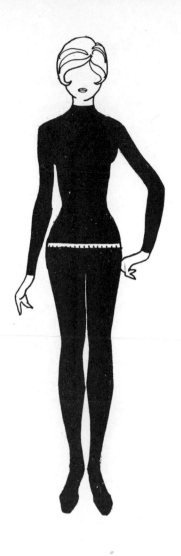

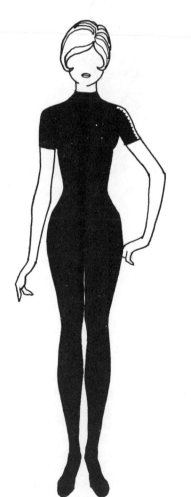

12. <u>Short Sleeve Length.</u> Measure from shoulder point to the desired length.

13. <u>3/4 Sleeve Length.</u> Measure from the shoulder point 4" below the elbow.

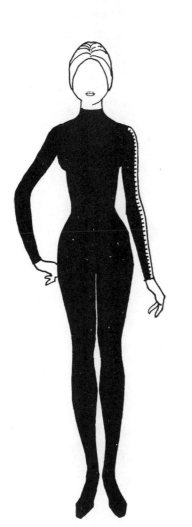

14. <u>Long Sleeve Length.</u> Measure from shoulder point past the elbow to the thin part of the wrist.

15. <u>Upper Arm</u>. Measure loosely the thickest part of the upper arm.

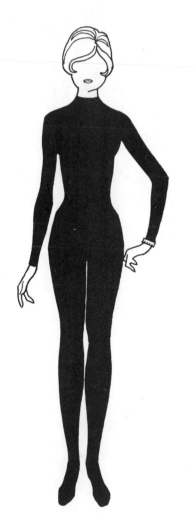

16. <u>Wrist</u>. Measure loosely around the wrist. Do not make this measurement smaller than the fist measurement or garment will not go over your hand. If you want to make the sleeve tight at the wrist, a slit should be made in the sleeve.

17. <u>Palm.</u> Make the hand into a fist, measure from thumb knuckle across other knuckles around to the thumb knuckle.

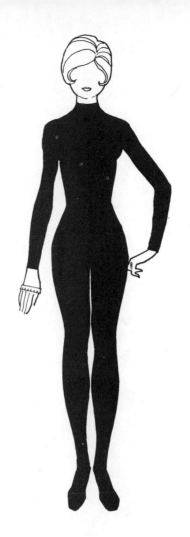

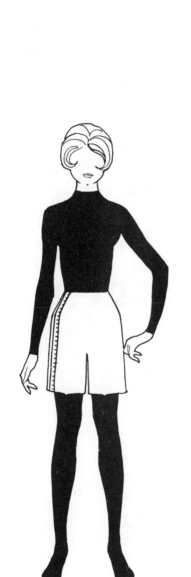

18. <u>Shorts Length.</u> Measure from the waist line down to the point on the leg where the middle finger touches the leg when the arm is placed along the side of the body.

19. <u>Slacks Length.</u> Measure from the waist down to the ankle.

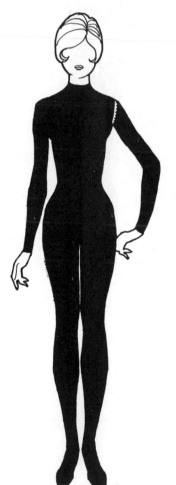

20. <u>Armhole.</u> Extend the arm slightly bent at the elbow to the side, measure around the armhole and add 2".

21. <u>Entire Back Length.</u> Measure from the most prominent vertebra at base of neck down to the back of the knee.

22. <u>Long Evening Dress Length.</u> Measure from the most prominent vertebra at base of neck down to the ankle.

23. <u>Side Bust Dart</u>. Subtract the front waist length from the back waist length to determine the width of the bust dart. Using the measurements from the chart on page 15:

Front waist length - 17-1/2"

Back waist length = 16"

The difference is 1-1/2".

Consequently, the side bust dart will be 1-1/2" wide.

24. <u>Front Waist Dart</u>. Follow the formula, <u>waist measurement divided by 8</u> to determine position of the front waist dart. Using the measurements from the chart:

Waist = 28" divided by 8 = 3-1/2"

The front waist dart will be 3-1/2" over from the center front.

25. <u>Bust tip</u>. Measure bust tip to bust tip and divide by 2. Generally, the measurement is 8" from bust tip to bust tip and divided by 2 would equal 4". On the front torso the bust tip would be 4" over from the center front line.

Chart of Women's Measurements-Medium Size

Part of Body	inch	Formulas inch
1. Neck	14-1/2	N ÷ 6 = 2-3/8
2. Shoulder	15-1/2	S ÷ 2 = 7-3/4
3. Front Width	14	FW ÷ 2 = 7
4. Back Width	14-1/2	BW ÷ 2 = 7-1/4
5. Bust Point	10	
6. Bust	36	B ÷ 4 = 9
7. Waist	28	W ÷ 4 = 7
8. Back Waist Length	16	
9. Front Waist Length	17-1/2	
10. Skirt Length	24	
11. Hip	38	H ÷ 4 = 9-1/2
12. Short Sleeve Length	8	
13. 3/4 Sleeve Length	16	
14. Long Sleeve Length	22	
15. Upper Arm	12	
16. Wrist	8	
17. Palm	10	
18. Shorts Length	16	
19. Slacks Length	38	
20. Armhole (Sleeveless)	16	
(With Sleeves)	18-1/2	
21. Entire Back Length (dress length)	40	
22. Long Evening Dress Length	54	

<u>Chart of Women's Measurements - Medium Size</u> (Continued)

Part of Body	inch	cm.	Formulas inch	cm.
23. Side Bust Dart	1-1/2	3.75		
24. Front Waist Dart	28÷8=3-1/2	8.75	W÷8=3-1/2	8.75
25. Bust Tip	8	20	BT÷2=4	10

Inches-Centimeter Conversion Chart

inches	cm.	inches	cm.	inches	cm.	inches	cm.	inches	cm.
1/8	0.3	2-3/8	6	9	22.5	27	67.5	45	112.5
1/4	0.6	2-1/2	6.3	10	25	28	70	46	115
3/8	1	2-5/8	6.6	11	27.5	29	72.5	47	117.5
1/2	1.3	2-3/4	6.9	12	30	30	75	48	120
5/8	1.6	2-7/8	7.3	13	32.5	31	77.5	49	122.5
3/4	1.9	3	7.5	14	35	32	80	50	125
7/8	2.3	3-1/8	7.8	15	37.5	33	82.5	51	127.5
1	2.5	3-1/4	8.1	16	40	34	85	52	130
1-1/8	2.8	3-3/8	8.5	17	42.5	35	87.5	53	132.5
1-1/4	3.1	3-1/2	8.8	18	45	36	90	54	135
1-3/8	3.5	3-5/8	9.1	19	47.5	37	92.5	55	137.5
1-1/2	3.8	3-3/4	9.4	20	50	38	95	56	140
1-5/8	4.1	3-7/8	9.8	21	52.5	39	97.5	57	142.5
1-3/4	4.4	4	10	22	55	40	100	58	145
1-7/8	4.8	5	12.5	23	57.5	41	102.5	59	147.5
2	5	6	15	24	60	42	105	60	150
2-1/8	5.3	7	17.5	25	62.5	43	107.5	61	152.2
2-1/4	5.6	8	20	26	65	44	110	62	155

Your Personal Measurement Chart

Part of Body	inch	Formulas inch
1. Neck		$N \div 6 =$
2. Shoulder		$S \div 2 =$
3. Front Width		$FW \div 2 =$
4. Back Width		$BW \div 2 =$
5. Bust Point		
6. Bust		$B \div 4 =$
7. Waist		$W \div 4 =$
8. Back Waist Length		
9. Front Waist Length		
10. Skirt Length		
11. Hip		$H \div 4 =$
12. Short Sleeve Length		
13. 3/4 Sleeve Length		
14. Long Sleeve Length		
15. Upper Arm		
16. Wrist		
17. Palm		
18. Shorts Length		
19. Slacks Length		
20. Armhole (Sleeveless) (With Sleeves)		
21. Entire Back Length		
22. Long Evening Dress Length		
23. Side Bust Dart		
24. Front Waist Dart		
25. Bust Tip		

Supplies Needed for Patternless Fashion Design

1. Straight ruler - 18"

2. Sharp metal instrument to mark

   darts on material

3. Scissors

4. Pinking Shears

5. Tool to Cut Buttonholes

6. Curved Ruler

7. Pressing Mitts

8. Square Ruler

9. Chalk Pencil

10. Tape Measure

11. Straight Pins

12. Iron

13. Pattern Paper

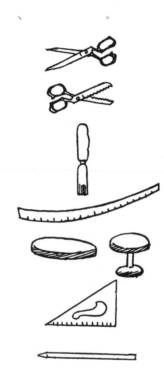

Meaning of Markings Throughout the Book

Seam Line (darker than guide line)

Guide Line

Fold

Fold Line

Fold Facing Line

Equal Spacing Mark

Square Mark - Right Angle

Grain Mark

Bias

Pleat Mark - bring fold line to other

line indicated by arrow.

Notch

Easing Mark

Fold and Cut Open

Extend

Marking to denote where lines cross

Mark meaning to cut along pattern

Box Pleat Mark

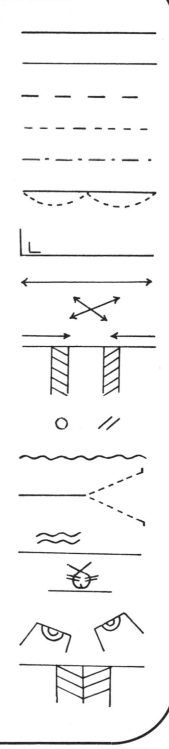

Abbreviations Used Throughout this Book

N.P.	=	Neck Point
S.P.	=	Shoulder Point
F.W.	=	Front Width
B.W.	=	Back Width
B.P.	=	Bust Point
W.L.	=	Waist Line
F.L.	=	Fold Line
H.	=	Hip
B.L.	=	Bust Line
A.H.	=	Armhole
K.L.	=	Knee Line

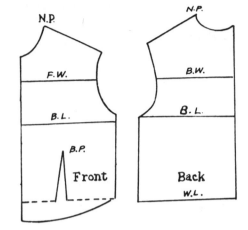

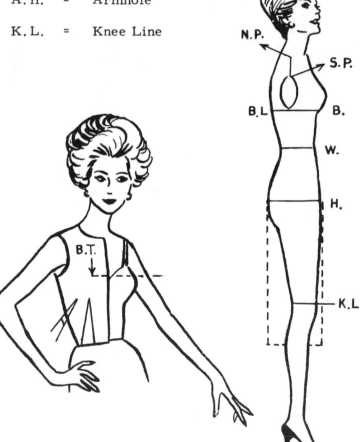

Now is the time to reveal the secret of how to make clothes without a pattern by marking directly on the fabric with tailors chalk. The measurements on page 15 have been used throughout the book for demonstrating purposes. The four easy steps for drawing on the fabric are the following:

1. Measure the widest part of the body -- either bust or hip.

2. Fold the fabric (lengthwise) the width equal to either the bust or hip measurement (whichever is wider) divided by 4 plus 1" seams.

3. Save 1" at the top of the fabric for seams and 3" at the bottom of the torso for the hem.

4. Fold the shoulder, bust, and small armhole dart in the middle and pin on the dart lines before marking the 1" seam allowance around the torso.

The measurements used in the accompanying drawings are:

Hip = 38"

Bust = 36"

38" divided by 4 = 9-1/2" + 1" = 10-1/2"

Fold the fabric lengthwise 10-1/2" wide, the same width all along the length. Start measuring from the fold side of the fabric so the grain lines will be correct. Styles drawn on the bias will be indicated by this (⋈) mark. Draw the front torso, neck, shoulder, and bust line with tailors chalk. When the front torso is completed, fold the remaining width if there is enough fabric, and draw the back torso. If there is not enough fabric left in the width to draw the back torso (there may not be in 36" width fabric), draw it below the front.

Collars, sleeves, and belt may be drawn in the remaining width if there is not enough to draw the back. These pieces may also be drawn below the torso.

The whole purpose of this classic technique is to teach how styles can be adapted or copied to present or past designs.

The Chinese have used these few basic techniques for centuries to create any design that is fashionable. The technique, therefore, can never be outdated.

These illustrations show how to draw the front and back torso and a skirt on the material. The dotted lines indicate the seam allowance added after the torso is drawn.

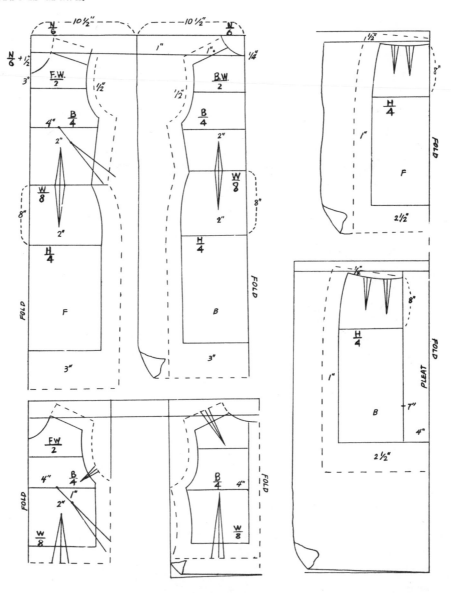

2

Front & Back Torso

Method of Drawing the Front Torso

The formula to follow when drawing the neck

front is:

Neck measurement divided by 6

Using the measurements from the chart on

page 15: Neck 14-1/2" divided by 6" = 2-3/8"

Shoulder 15-1/2" divided by 2 = 7-3/4"

When drawing the front torso draw a right

angle line (⌐) with the corner facing the

upper left.   The vertical line will be the

center front line and the horizontal line

will be the basic shoulder line.

When drawing the back torso pattern, the

right angle will be drawn with the corner

facing to the right.

To draw the front neck line, measure down

from the corner on the vertical line 2-3/8"

plus 1/2".   Measure over from the corner

on the horizontal line 2-3/8", connect these

two measurements forming a square.   On

the corner of the square measure in 3/4"

and make a curve touching the 3/4" point.

Measure across the shoulder line 7-3/4".

At this measurement, draw a straight line

down 2".   Connect the 2" point to the

neck point or the 2-3/8" measurement

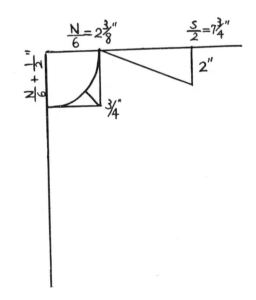

previously drawn.

The formula to follow to determine the front width is:

<u>Front width measurement divided by 2</u>

Using the measurement from the chart on page 15, <u>front width = 14" divided by 2 = 7".</u> To draw the front width line, measure down 3" from the neck opening and draw a line across 7". This 7" is half of the front width.

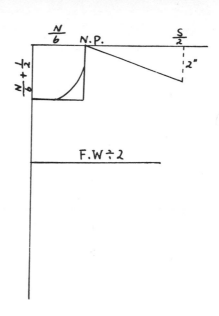

The bust point position is determined by measuring from the neck point down the center front line 10". The standard bust point measurement from the chart on page 15 is 10". The bust line in the picture, therefore, is drawn at this 10" point.

The formula to follow to determine the length of the bust line is:

<u>Bust measurement divided by 4</u>

The bust measurement in the chart is 36" divided by 4 = 9".

Starting at the 10" point on the center front line draw a straight line across the pattern 9" long for the bust line. At the end of the center front line, draw a line across the torso and up to the bust line.

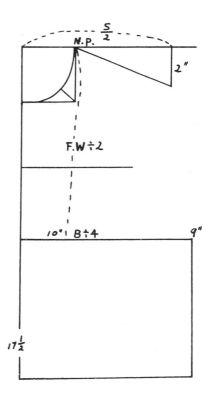

Front Waist Length

Sometimes the front waistline length is longer than the back waistline length. Subtract the shorter of the two lengths from the longer to determine this difference. Using the measurements in the chart:

Front waistline length = 17-1/2"

Back waistline length = 16"

The difference is 1-1/2". This 1-1/2" must be added at the bottom of the waistline at the center front. Refer to the drawing.

Armhole

The formula to follow to determine the size of the armhole is:

armhole measurement divided by 2

The sleeveless armhole measurement in the chart is 16" divided by 2 = 8". Always use the sleeveless measurement for figuring the torso. To draw the armhole, extend the underarm line up from the bust line and connect the shoulder point to the front width line. Make a deep curve to connect the front width line to the underarm point. To measure the armhole when drawing, place the tape measure on edge. Start at the shoulder point and touch

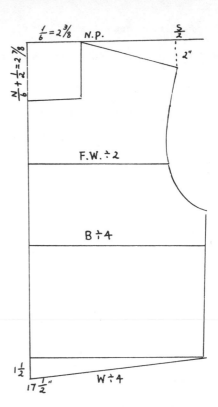

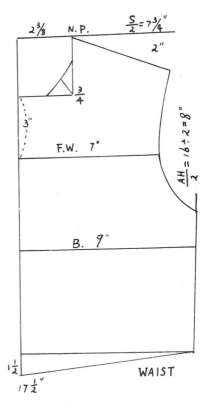

the front width line. Make a mark on the torso to equal the armhole measurement on the extended underarm line. Be sure to curve the line from the front width to the underarm measurement. After drawing the armhole check with a tape measurement to be certain that this armhole equals armhole measurement divided by 2.

Front Waistline Dart

The formula to determine the position of the front waistline dart is:

<u>Waistline measurement divided by 8</u>

Using the measurements from the chart on page 15, study the equation, 28" divided by 8 = 3-1/2" on the waistline, and make a mark for the dart. Make another mark 1/2" over from this mark, and another mark 1/2" beyond that. On the second 1/2" mark, draw a straight line up to a point 2" below the bust point. Finish making the dart by connecting the 1/2" mark on the waistline to the top of the dart line 2" down from the bust point.

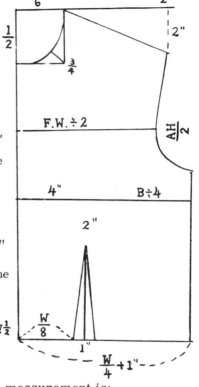

The formula to follow to determine the waist length measurement is:

<u>Waistline measurement divided by 4 + 1" (dart)</u>

Using this formula and the measurement from the chart, 28" divided by 4 plus 1" = 8". Make a mark 8" from the center front line across the waistline. Fold the waist dart on the dart line, and connect the waistline point with a curved ruler (curve of the ruler inward) to the armhole.

The formula to determine the bust point is:

<u>Measure from the center front line across the bust line 4"</u>

This 4" is the bust point.

To finish making this dart, extend the waistline one inch and connect this extension to the 4" bust point. Draw a straight line from underarm to waist measurement at the point where this line crosses the dart line. Measure 1-1/2" for width of the dart. Measure down 1" from the bust point and connect this measurement to 1-1/2" width mark with a straight line continuing this line to the underarm front torso line. Refer to the drawing.

Fold the dart and use the curved ruler (curve inward) to draw a line connecting the underarm to the waist.

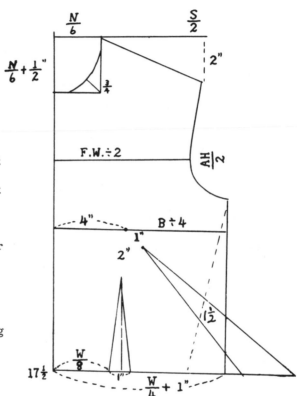

This drawing refers to the women's measurements chart on page 15. To draw the neck opening for everyone, the formula to follow when making the original pattern is:

$$\frac{S}{2} = 7\frac{3}{4} \qquad \frac{N}{6} = 2\frac{3}{8}$$

 <u>Neck measurement divided by 6</u>

To draw the shoulder for everyone the formula to follow is:

 <u>shoulder length divided by 2</u>

Shoulder 15-1/2" divided by 2 = 7-3/4"

Neck 14-1/2" divided by 6 = 2-3/8"

Draw a right angle line (⌐). The vertical line will be the back center line (fold line) and the horizontal line will be the basic shoulder line. The neck line is drawn in a curve from the corner of the right angle with a mark 1/4" down on the vertical line and 2-3/8" across the horizontal line as shown in the drawing above. Mark across 7-3/4" on the top line from the corner of the right angle, and from here draw a 1-1/2" line at a right angle. At the 2-3/8" point, draw a line up 1/2", and connect this point to the 1-1/2" shoulder point with a straight line.

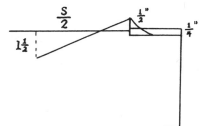

Back Waist Length

The back waist length from the chart equals 16". On the center back line, measure down 16" from the neck 1/4" mark. From this line, draw a horizontal line to the left at a right angle.

Back Width

The formula for drawing the back width line
for everyone is:

Back width measurement divided by 2

On the center back line mark down 5" from the
center back neck 1/4". This 5" measurement
is used to determine the position of the back
width line for everyone regardless of size.
The back width measurement in the drawing
is 14-1/2" divided by 2 = 7-1/4".

Draw the back width line down 5" from the
neck and across 7-1/4".

Back Bust Line

The back bust line position is 10" down from
the neck, regardless of size. Measure down
the center back line from shoulder line at the
neck and draw the line across 9". This 9"
line is the same measurement as the front
bust measurement from the chart on page 15.

Back Waistline

To draw the back waistline, measure down
the center back from the 1/4" up point and
draw a line the length of the back waist length
measurement (16" in this drawing).

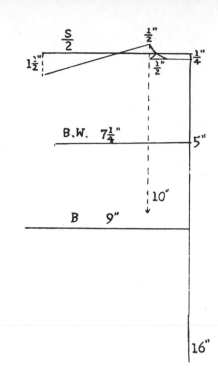

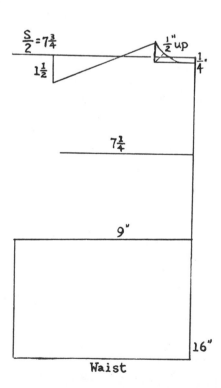

Waist

To draw the armhole, connect the shoulder point to the back width line. Make a deep curve from back width to the back underarm, using the tape measure to make the armhole measurement and following the same procedure used when drawing the armhole for the front waist.

Back Waist Dart

To determine the position of the back waistline dart, use the following formula:

Waistline measurement divided by 8

Draw the waistline dart in the back waist, following the same procedure learned for the front waist dart. Waist measurement in the chart is 28" divided by 8 = 3-1/2".

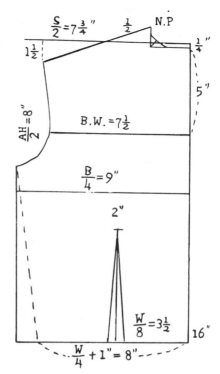

The lower drawing shows the back and front torso finished. The dotted lines indicate seam allowances to be added to the torso before cutting.

A front and back original torso may be made in cardboard. Place the cardboard torsos on the material, draw around them with tailors chalk. Changes for various styles may then be made directly on the fabric on the original torsos.

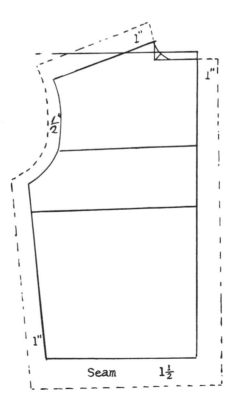

The illustrations below show the front and back torso from two different angles.

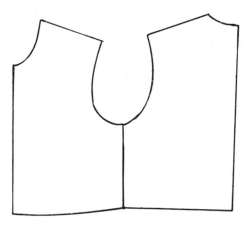

Now you have learned how to draft a front and back torso from medium size measurements. Practice drafting these torsos using different measurements, your own and your friends. The more you practice the quicker you will find how easy it is to draw torsos for different measurements.

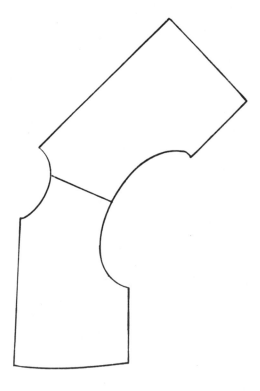

The illustrations below identify blouse front, blouse back, skirt front, skirt back and also indicate basic formulas, width of darts, as well as areas to be trimmed away because of torso changes. (~~LEFT~~)

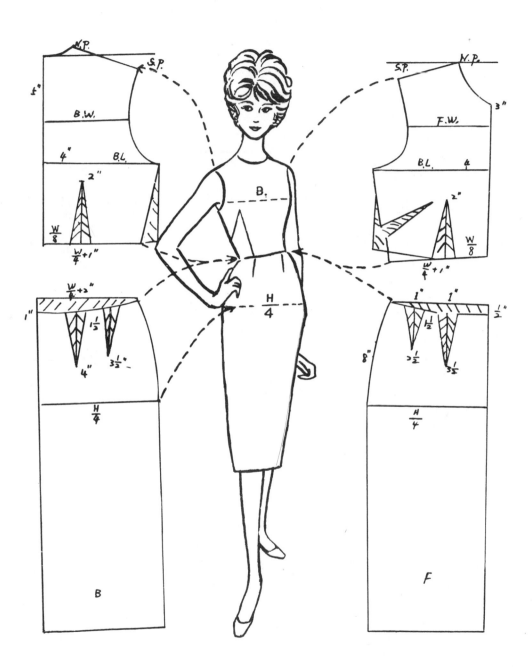

The illustrations below show the various positions of darts on the front and back torso.

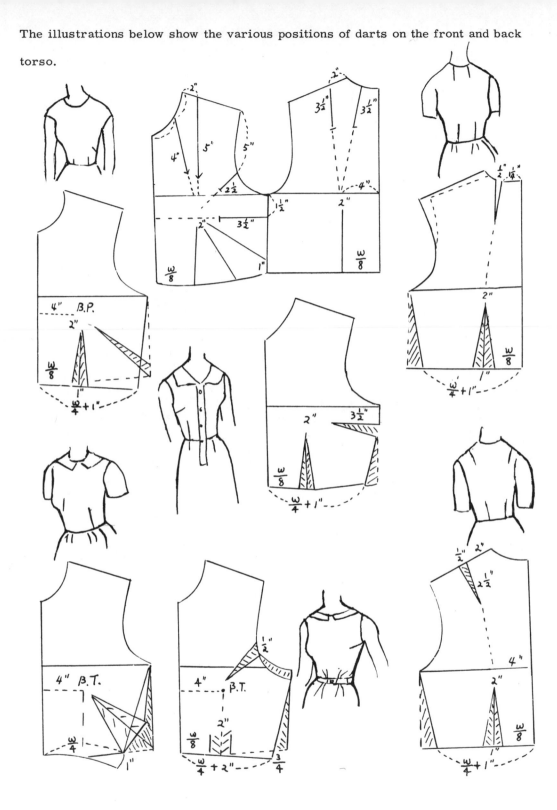

3

Fabric Requirements

Fabric Requirements

To determine the amount of fabric to purchase, 4" must always be added to the requirements regardless of size (1" for shoulder seam allowance and 3" for hem). Purchase 1/2 yard of fabric for all collar styles except the sailor collar, which requires 3/4 yard of material.

Purchase one long sleeve length for long sleeve styles, and one 3/4 sleeve length for 3/4 sleeve styles. Short sleeves can usually be cut from the width, but if there is not enough width left in the fabric, add 10" for short sleeves.

To determine the required width, use the largest measurement (hip or bust). The skirt band is cut from the remaining width.

To make a dress from checked fabric, or fabric with a nap such as velvet or corduroy, buy 1/4 yard more fabric.

Fabric Requirements for Skirts

Fabric 36", 44", or 54" wide requirements for the <u>straight skirt</u>, <u>A-line</u>, <u>six-gore</u>, and <u>skirt with a center front pleat</u> are:

<u>2 skirt lengths plus 8"</u> (3" hem each skirt length + 1" seam at skirt top) for all sizes.

<u>Circle or Flare Style Skirts -- Fabric Requirements</u>
Fabric 36", 44", or 54" wide requirements for the circle or flare style skirt are:

<u>skirt length plus 1/4 yard for all sizes</u>
After cutting the skirt from 54" wide fabric there will be much fabric left in the width which can be used to make a vest or over-blouse.

72" wide felt fabric requirements for the circle skirt are:

> one skirt length + 9" for all sizes.

Fabric Requirements for the Gathered Skirt

36" wide fabric requirements for all sizes are:

> waist measurement times 3

Using the measurements from the chart, 28" x 3 - 84"

> 84" divided by 36" wide fabric = 2-1/3 yards.

44" wide fabric requirements for all sizes are:

> two skirt lengths plus 8" for hem

54" wide fabric requirements for all sizes are:

> 1-1/2 yards

This 54" width is wide enough to cut two lengths by folding the fabric lengthwise.

Fabric Requirements for the Blouse

Front waist length plus 1" (shoulder) plus 4" (length for overblouse) plus 2" hem. The tuck in blouse requires 6" instead of 4".

36" wide fabric requirements for all sizes are:

> two front waist lengths plus the other
>
> additions (7")

44" wide fabric requirements for all sizes are:

> one front waist length plus the additions

Fabric Requirements for Slacks and Shorts

36" or 44" fabric requirements for all sizes

are:

two desired lengths plus 3"

54" wide fabric requirements for all sizes

are:

one desired length

Fabric Requirements for the Shift Dress

36" or 39" wide fabric requirements are:

If the largest measurement is smaller than

36", purchase one length of fabric plus 4".

If the largest measurement is larger than

36", purchase two lengths of fabric plus 4".

44" wide fabric requirements are:

If the largest measurement is smaller than

44", purchase two lengths of fabric plus 4".

54" wide fabric requirements are:

Buy one dress length of fabric plus 4" for

all sizes.

Fabric Requirements for the Cut Waist Style Dress

To determine the amount of fabric to purchase for all sizes, add the front waist length measurement plus 6", plus the skirt length measurement.

Follow the directions previously given for sleeve styles.

Using the medium size measurements from the chart:

the front waist length = 17-1/2"

plus 6" (1" for shoulder seam, 1" for

      waistline seam, 1" for skirt top

      seam, and 3" for hem)

plus the skirt length 24" = 47-1/2"

36" wide fabric requirements for the cut waist style:

If the largest measurement is smaller than 36", purchase one length of material plus 6".

If the largest measurement is larger than 36", purchase two lengths of material plus 6."

44" wide fabric requirements:

If the largest measurement is smaller than 44", purchase one length of material plus 6".

If the largest measurement is larger than 44", purchase two lengths of fabric plus 6".

54" wide fabric requirements:

Purchase one dress length of fabric plus 6" regardless of size.

Maternity Dress Fabric Requirements

36" or 44" wide fabric requirements for all sizes are:

two dress lengths plus 4" seams

54" wide fabric requirements for all sizes are:

one dress length plus 4" seams

Maternity Blouse Fabric Requirements

36" or 44" wide fabric requirements for all sizes are:

two blouse lengths plus 3" seams

54" wide fabric requirements for all sizes are:

one blouse length plus 3" seams

Maternity Skirt Fabric Requirements

36" wide fabric requirements for all sizes are:

two skirt lengths plus 8" (hem + seams)

44" wide fabric requirements for all sizes are:

if largest measurement is smaller than 40", buy one skirt length plus 4".

If largest measurement is larger than 40", buy two skirt lengths plus 8".

54" wide fabric requirements for all sizes are:

one skirt length plus 4"

Evening Dress Fabric Requirements

The fabric requirements are the same for all style

dresses and sizes.

36" wide fabric requirements are:

<u>one dress length plus 6"</u> -- 1" shoulder seam
2" waist seams and
skirt top
3" hem

44" wide fabric requirements are:

If the largest measurement is smaller than

40", buy one dress length plus 6".

If the largest measurement is larger than

40", buy two dress lengths plus 12".

Coat Fabric Requirements

36" wide fabric requirements for all sizes are:

<u>three coat lengths plus 8"</u>

The extra width left over after cutting will be enough

to cut the collar, and long, 3/4 or short sleeves.

44" wide fabric requirements for all sizes are:

<u>two coat lengths plus 8" plus 3/4 yard for</u>

<u>long, 3/4, or short sleeves.</u>

The collar can be cut from the extra width left after

cutting.

54" wide fabric requirements for all sizes are:

<u>two coat lengths plus 8"</u>

It is not necessary to buy more for collar or sleeves,

the extra width will cut these pieces.

Fabric Requirements for the Suit or Blouse and Skirt

The fabric requirements for the suit are the same as for the blouse and skirt. The fabric requirements are:

front waist length plus 13", plus the skirt length plus the sleeve length.

The 13" measurement includes the following:

shoulder seam allowance 1"

amount added to blouse length 6"

blouse hem 2"

skirt top seam 1"

skirt hem 3"

36" Wide Fabric Requirements

If the largest measurement is smaller than 36", purchase one length of fabric plus 13".

If the largest measurement is larger than 36", purchase two lengths of material plus 13".

44" Wide Fabric Requirements

If the largest measurement is smaller than 44", purchase one length of fabric plus 13".

If the largest measurement is larger than 44", purchase two lengths of fabric plus 13".

54" Wide Fabric Requirements

Measure the front waist length plus 13", plus the skirt length, plus the sleeve length.

Children's Dress Fabric Requirements

36", 44", or 54" wide fabric requirements

for all sizes are:

> one dress length plus 4" seams

Children's Skirt Fabric Requirements

Fabric requirements are the same as for adults.

Children's Blouse Fabric Requirements

Front waist length plus 3" (overblouse style or 5"

tuck-in style) plus 2" hem plus 1" shoulder seam.

(13" + 3" +3" = 19").   For collars and sleeves,

purchase 1/2 yard more fabric.

36" wide fabric requirements for all sizes:

19" plus 1/2 yard for collar and sleeves or buy

one yard of fabric.

44" wide fabric requirements are:

> 3/4 yard of fabric because the fabric

can be folded.

Children's Shorts Fabric Requirements

Shorts length plus 1" seams at waist plus 2" hem.

36" or 44" fabric requirements are:

> two shorts lengths plus the additions.

Children's Slacks Fabric Requirements

Slacks length plus 1" seam at waist plus 2" hem.

36" or 44" wide fabric requirements are:

> two slack lengths plus additions.

4

Sleeves

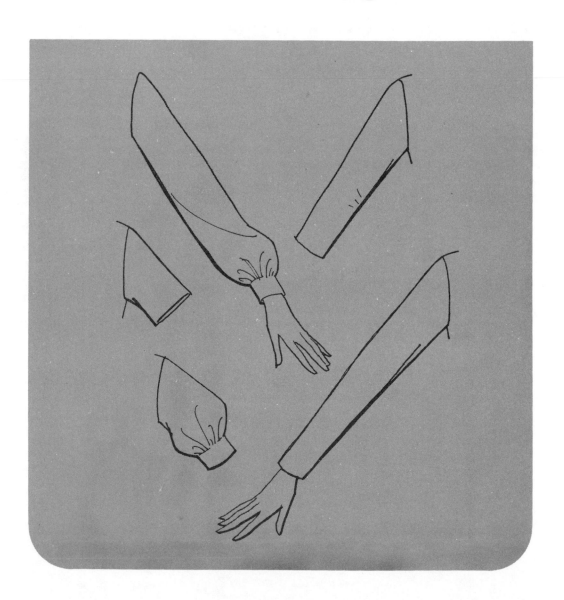

The sleeve shown is used for blouses, dresses and coats. The measurements from the chart on page 15 were used in these drawings. The sleeve lengths are as follows:

Long sleeve length, 22"

Short sleeve length 8"

The armhole measurement used is 18-1/2", which is the armhole measurement used for a garment with sleeves. The armhole measurement used for sleeve-less garments is 16". Note that the armhole measurement for a garment with sleeves is 2-1/2" larger than the armhole measurement for a sleeveless garment.

Method for Drafting Short Sleeve

Sleeve cap is determined by armhole measurement (18-1/2" divided by 4 + 1 = 5-3/8")

A to B = armhole divided by 2 = 9-1/4"

A to E + sleeve length = 8"

F to G = sleeve band = 13"

Connect A B F G C A to complete the drawing.

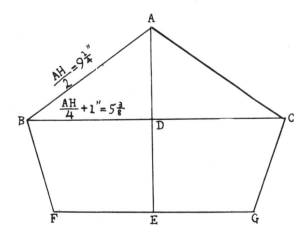

Right side of sleeve is front, left side of sleeve is the back in the drawings shown below.

Divide line AD into three parts. At back sleeve top, mark out 3/4" on first line and in 1/4" on second line.

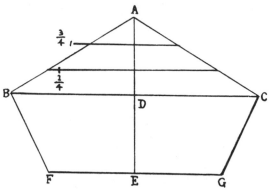

Draw around marks 3/4" and 1/4" and from A to B. At front sleeve top F mark out 3/4" on first line and mark in 1/2" on second line. Draw around these points from A to C.

Side view of short sleeve.

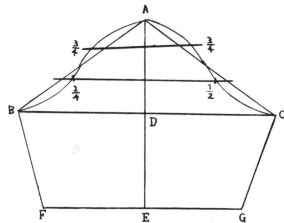

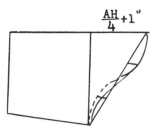

The method of drafting a long sleeve is the same as the method used for the short sleeve except for the difference in length. Using the chart measurements armhole 18-1/2" divided by 4 + 1 = 5-3/8" measurement for sleeve cap.

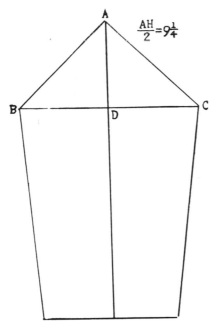

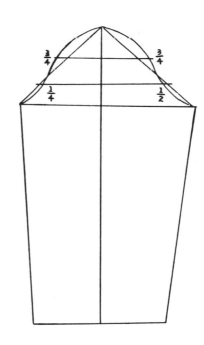

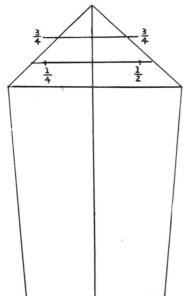

Slanting line to half the size of the armhole = 9-1/4"

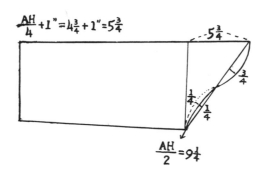

The formula used for figuring sleeve cap in a garment used for action is:

<u>5" down from sleeve top</u>

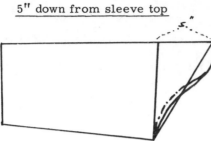

The formula used for figuring sleeve cap for a sleeve that looks nice, but is not

large enough for work or action is:

<u>5-1/2" down from sleeve top</u>

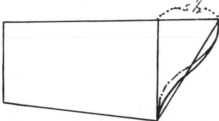

The formula used for figuring sleeve cap for a tight sleeve is:

<u>6" down from sleeve top</u>

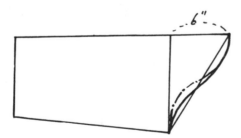

A regular sleeve is 8" long. These drawings show a regular sleeve. To draw this sleeve, refer to the method used earlier in the book for the basic short sleeve.

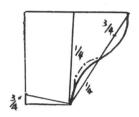
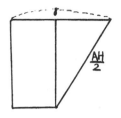

Puff Sleeve

Draw a regular short sleeve pattern, add 1" at the bottom underarm sleeve edge. Connect this line to the armhole. On the fold of the sleeve add 1-1/2" on the bottom edge of the sleeve and connect to the sleeve top. Add 1-1/2" in the middle of the bottom of the sleeve. Extend the fold line 1/2" longer.

Connect the 1-1/2" to the 1/2" extension on the fold edge and the 1" extension on underarm.

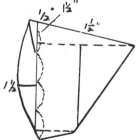

3/4 Puff Sleeve

Never draw a dart in a 3/4" sleeve. To draw the sleeve illustrated below, measure down on the fold edge of the sleeve 5-3/4" and draw a line across 7". The 3/4" sleeve length in the chart equals 16". The sleeve in the picture is made 15" and the band is 1" wide. Consequently the entire sleeve length will be 16" finished. Draw a line 7" across for the bottom of the sleeve. Draw the armhole sleeve curve as shown in previous drawings and connect to the sleeve bottom. At the center of the sleeve bottom draw a mark out 1". Draw a curved line from one edge of the sleeve touching this 1" mark to the other edge of the sleeve. Divide the second division in half and make a 2-1/2" long slit at this point.

Sleeve Band

Measure around the forearm at the position of the 3/4" length sleeve. Draw the sleeve band the length equal to the forearm measurement, and 3" wide.

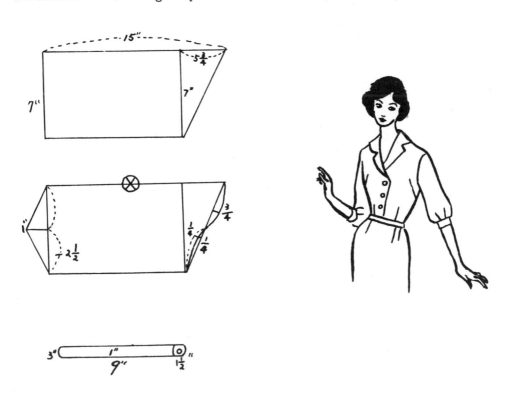

Long Sleeve with a Wrist Band

Draw a regular long sleeve. The entire length of
the long sleeve in the chart is 22". Draw the
sleeve 20" because the sleeve band folded is 2"
making the entire sleeve 22" long. Measure down
5-3/4" from the sleeve top, and draw a line across
7". The formula to follow to make the armhole is:

<u>armhole measurement divided by 2</u>

Following the 18-1/2" measurement from the chart,
18-1/2" divided by 2 = 9-1/4".

Draw a straight line 9-1/4" from the sleeve top to the
7" measurement. Divide this line into three equal parts.
At the first division, extend the mark 3/4" out and at
the second division draw the mark in 1/4". Draw a curved line starting at the
sleeve top, touching the 3/4" out point and the 1/4" in point, continue until joined
to the 7" mark at underarm edge. Divide the bottom of the sleeve into two equal
parts. At the division mark make a line 3/4" out. Extend the fold side of the
sleeve 1/2". Connect the underarm mark, touch the 3/4" point and the 1/2"
point. Divide the second division in half, and at this point draw a slit 3" long.

Band

The wrist measurement from the chart equals 8". Draw the sleeve band 8" long
plus 1" for button, and make the band 4" wide.

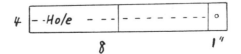

French Cuff

Any desired width cuff can be added to the bottom of a long sleeve. To make a french cuff, cut fabric 6" wide plus seam allowance (finished cuff width will be 3") for each sleeve. Cut interfacing 3" wide, baste to wrong side of fabric. Fold cuff in half and stitch around the edges leaving side to be attached to the sleeve open. Make a placket in the sleeve by slashing sleeve and stay-stitching the slash. Cut a piece of fabric 1" wide and the length of the slash plus seam allowance for the underlap of the sleeve back. Turn under seam allowances at outer edge. Pin underlap to slash on back of the sleeve right sides together, baste, stitch, turn to inside and stitch turned-in edge over seam. Cut a piece of fabric one inch wide and one inch longer than the slash for the front overlap. With right sides together pin this overlap piece to inside of front edge of sleeve, stitch, press seams toward facings. Turn overlap to right side and crease at fold line. Baste turned-in edge over seam. Lap placket and baste. Sew all around placket from the bottom up around the point and across the bottom. Gather bottom of sleeve to fit the cuff. Sew bottom of sleeve and one edge of cuff right sides together. Turn to inside, turn in seam allowance on cuff and hand stitch to sleeve. The french cuff may be top-stitched around the outside edges. Close with buttons and button-holes or make small buttonholes to be used with cuff links.

5

Necklines

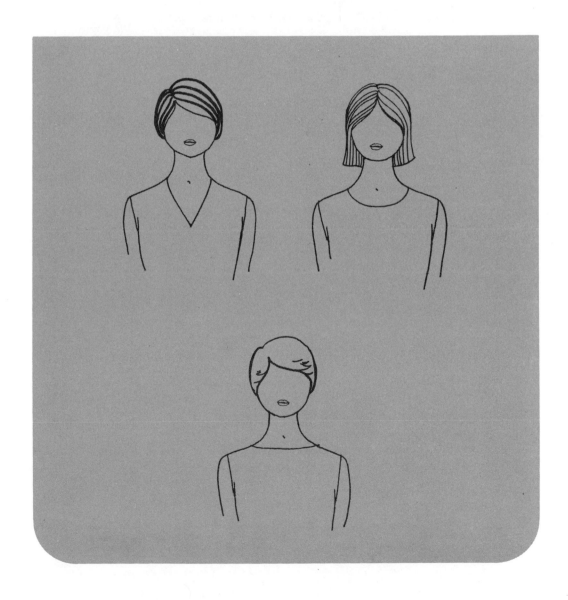

Necklines

Always allow 24" for measurement around the neck so the dress may be pulled over the head. Lines like (⬚) mean this portion of the torso should be trimmed away before torso is cut.

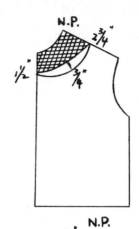

Round Neckline

Draw a front torso. Measure over from the neck point on the shoulder line 2-3/4". Measure down on the center front line from the neck 1-1/2". Connect the two points with a straight line. Divide this straight line in half. At the half mark, draw a line in 3/4". Draw a curved line connecting the 1-1/2", 3/4" and 2-3/4" marks.

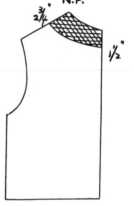

Draw a back torso. Measure across the shoulder line from the neck point 2-3/4". Measure down the center back 1-1/2" from the neck. With a curved line connect the 2-3/4" mark to the 1-1/2" mark.

The illustrations below show the finished torso unfolded.

F

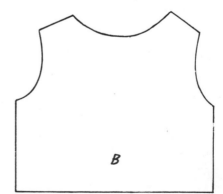

B

Low Round Neckline

Draw a front torso. Measure over from the neck point on the shoulder line 2-3/4". Measure down the center front line from the neck 2-1/2". Connect the 2-3/4" point to the 1-1/2" point with a curved line.

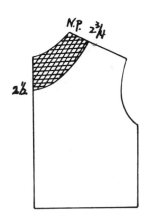

Draw a back torso. Measure across 2-3/4" from the neck point on the shoulder line. Measure down from the center front neck 1-1/2". Connect these two points with a curved line.

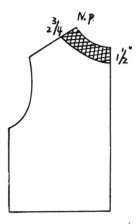

The illustrations below show the front and back torsos unfolded.

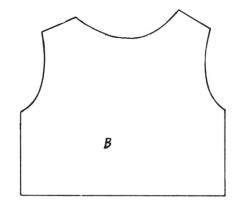

V Neckline

The formula for drawing a V neckline is:

Measure from the bust line up 1-1/4"

Draw a front torso. Divide the shoulder line into three equal parts. Measure from the bust line up 1-1/4". Connect this mark to the first division mark made at the shoulder.

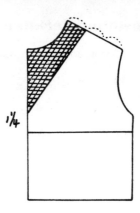

Draw a back torso. Divide the shoulder line into three equal parts. Divide the line from the center back neck to the back bust line into two equal parts. Connect this mark to the first division mark made at the shoulder.

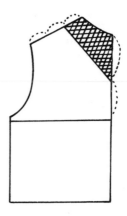

The two illustrations below show the finished torso pieces unfolded.

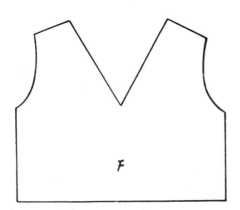

F

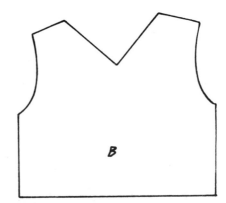

B

Square Neckline

Draw a front torso. Measure over from the neck point 1-3/4"
on the shoulder line. Measure down the center front
1-1/2" from the center front neck. Draw a straight
line down from the 1-3/4" mark on the shoulder across
to the 1-1/2" on the center front. From the square,
measure in 1/2" and connect this 1/2" measurement
to the 1-3/4" point on the shoulder.

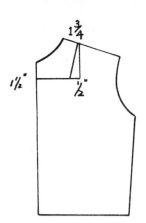

Draw a back torso. Measure down the center back
fold line 1-1/2" from the center back neck. Measure
over from the neck point on the shoulder 1-3/4". Connect
these two marks with a curved line.

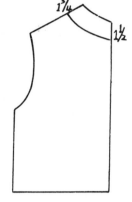

The drawings below show the front and back torso unfolded.

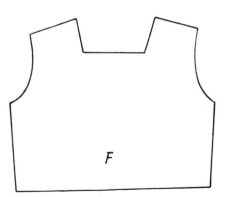

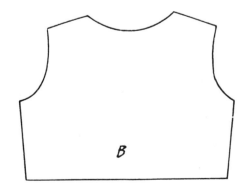

Square V Neckline

Draw a front torso. At the neck point make a mark over 2-1/2" on the shoulder line. Divide the line from the bust line to the center front neck into four equal parts. At the second division on the center front line, draw a line across 3-1/2", connect to the 2-1/2" mark on the shoulder. On the center front line at the third division, draw a line to the 3-1/2" point.

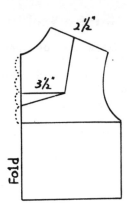

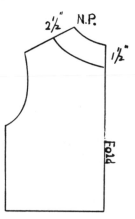

Draw a back torso. Measure down 1-1/2" on the center back line from the neck. Measure from the neck point across the shoulder line 2-1/2". Connect these two points with a curved line.

The two drawings below show the front and back torsos unfolded. The drawings above show the front and back torsos on the fold.

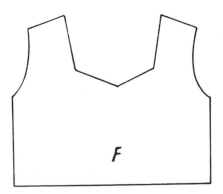

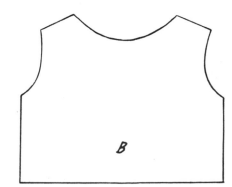

Draw a front torso.   Measure up 1/2" from center front neck.   Measure from neck point over on shoulder line 3".   Lower shoulder at armhole edge 1/2". Connect the 1/2" at the neck to the 3" over on the shoulder to the 1/2" lower shoulder line.

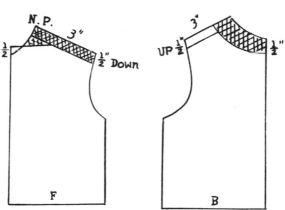

Draw a back torso.   Measure from neck point over on shoulder line 3". Raise the shoulder at armhole edge 1/2".   The front shoulder was lowered so it is necessary to raise the back shoulder.   Connect the three points.

The drawings below show the finished torso pieces unfolded.

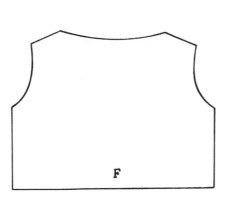

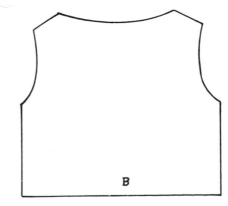

Sweetheart Neckline

Draw a front torso. Measure over on the shoulder line 2-3/4" from the neck point as shown in the picture. Measure up 1-1/4" from the bust line. Connect the neck point and the 1-1/4" mark with a straight line. Divide the straight line into three equal parts. At the first division make a mark in 3/4", at the second division make the mark 1/4" out. With a curved line connect the marks.

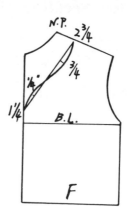

Draw a back torso. Measure across the shoulder line 2-3/4" from the neck point. Measure down the center back line from the neck 1-1/2". With a curved line, connect the 2-3/4" point to the 1-1/2" point.

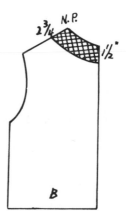

The drawings below show the completed torsos unfolded.

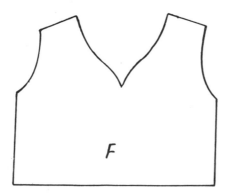

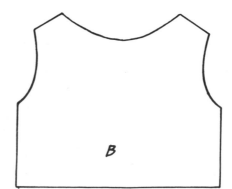

6

Collars

Here are the directions for five different collars:

Square Style Collar

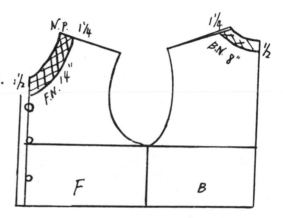

Draw a front torso. Measure over from the neck point on the shoulder line 1-1/4". Measure from the neck down the center front 1-1/2". Connect these two points, and trim out the extra.

Back

To draw the back neck, measure from the neck point over on the shoulder line 1-1/4". Measure from the neck at the center back down 1/2". Connect these two points.

Collar

The formula to follow to determine the collar length is:

<u>front neck measurement plus back</u>

<u>neck measurement divided by 2</u>

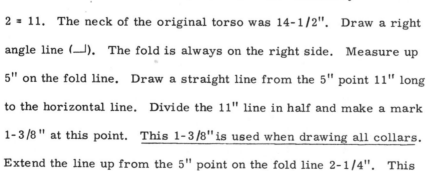

In the drawing, the front neck measurment is 14", and the back neck measurement is 8", 14" + 8" = 22" divided by 2 = 11. The neck of the original torso was 14-1/2". Draw a right angle line (⌐⌐). The fold is always on the right side. Measure up 5" on the fold line. Draw a straight line from the 5" point 11" long to the horizontal line. Divide the 11" line in half and make a mark 1-3/8" at this point. <u>This 1-3/8" is used when drawing all collars.</u> Extend the line up from the 5" point on the fold line 2-1/4". This 2-1/4" is the collar width. Draw a curved line from the 5" point connecting to the 11" measurement on the horizontal line touching the

1-3/8" point.   Draw a right angle line 2-1/2" up from the 11" point.

Connect this 2-1/2" point to the 2-1/4" point with a curved line.   Be

certain the width is 2-1/4" all along the collar.   Add 1/2" seam all

around the collar before cutting.

Wide Square Style Collar

Draw a front and back torso. Measure over from the neck point on the shoulder line 1-1/4", measure from the neck down on the center front 1-1/2". Connect these two points to draw the neck.

<u>Back</u>

Measure from the neck point over on the shoulder line 1-1/4".

Measure from the neck at the center back down 1/2".

Connect these two points to complete the neck used

for this style collar.

<u>Collar</u>

To determine the length of the collar

follow the formula, <u>F.N. + B.N.</u> divided by 2.

(10 + 6-1/2) divided by 2 = 8-1/4".

Draw a right angle line (⌐). Measure up

2-3/4", extend the line 3" because this

collar is 3" wide. Draw this line across

4". Draw a 7" line down to touch the horizontal line. Draw a line up

4-1/2". Connect this 4-1/2" line to the 4" point with a straight line.

At the 4-1/2" point extend this line 1-1/2" and connect to the

horizontal line. Trim out the points at the top and bottom of

the collar by drawing curved lines. Refer to the drawing.

The regular torso neck has been made higher so it is neces-

sary to measure the front neck and back neck to determine

the collar length. The F.N. = 10", B.N. = 6-1/2" in this drawing hence

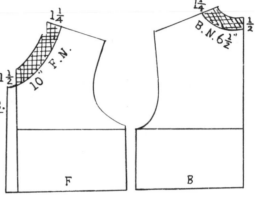

Star Point Collar

the collar length was figured 8-1/4" in the preceding equation.

Star Point Style Collar

Draw the front and back torso on the material. To draw
the neck, measure over from the neck point on the shoulder
line 1-1/4". Measure from the neck down the center
front 1-1/2". Connect these two points and trim out
the extra.

Back

To draw the back neck, measure from the neck point over
on the shoulder line 1-1/4". Measure from the neck
at the center back down 1/2". Connect these two points.

Collar

Draw a right angle (⌐) line. Measure up 5".
Extend this line 2-3/4" for the collar width.
Draw a straight line from the 5" point
11" long (F.N. + B.N.) divided by 2 to the horizontal line. Divide the 11" line in half
and make a mark 1-3/8" at this point.
At the 11" point on the horizontal line,
extend this line 2-1/2". Make a mark up 3/4". Make
another mark up 1-3/4" from the 3/4" point. Make
another measurement up 1/2" from the 1-3/4". Connect
the 1/2" point with a curved line to the 2-3/4" point on
the fold line. At the 1-3/4" mark draw a line in 1-1/4". Connect all these
lines to form the star point, 2-1/2" to the 3/4" to the 1-1/4" to the 1/2".
The medium torso neck measurement from the chart on page 15 is 14-1/2".

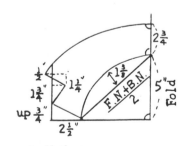

If the neck is cut lower or higher the neck measurement changes. It is necessary to measure the front neck and the back neck after the torso neck is changed. Then follow the formula, F. N. + B. N. divided by 2 = length of collar.

Sailor Collar with Tie

Draw a front and back torso. The yoke or width of this collar is 5". Measure over from the neck point on shoulder line 1-1/4". Measure from the neck down the center front 1-1/2". Connect these two points, and trim out the extra. Measure around the torso from the neck at the center front to the neck point to determine the collar length. This neck is cut lower so F. N. = 14" B. N. =8.

Back

Measure from neck point over on the shoulder line 1-1/4". Measure from neck at center back down 1/2". Connect these two points.

Collar

Draw a right angle line (⌐). Measure up 5" on the fold line, extend this line 4-1/4". Draw a straight line from the 5" point 11" long to the horizontal line. Extend the horizontal line 1-1/4". Draw a line from the 4-1/4" point across 5". Connect the 4-1/4" extension on the horizontal line to the 5" width line with a straight line. Make a mark up 1/2" on this line, and connect to the 1-1/4" point. Divide the straight line from the 5" width to the 1/2" up in half. At the half point make a mark in 1/4". Curve this line

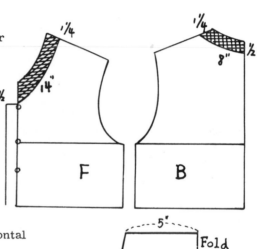

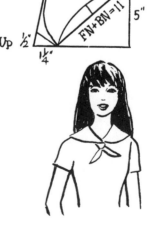

as shown in the picture down to the 1-1/4" point. Trim out the excess.
Be sure to divide the 11" line in half, and make a mark in 1-3/8" at this
point. Connect the 5" point to the 11" point touching the 1-3/8" mark to
curve the collar.

Peter Pan Style Collar

Draw a front and back torso. To draw the neck, measure over on the shoulder
line 1-1/4" from the neck point. Measure down the
center front from the neck 1-1/2". Connect these
two points.

Back

To draw the back neck, measure from neck point
over on the shoulder line 1-1/4". Measure from
neck at center back down 1/2". Connect these
two points.

Collar

Draw a right angle line (⌐). Measure up
on the fold line 5". Extend this line 3".
Draw a straight line from the 5" point 11"
long to the horizontal line. This 11" is
determined by using the formula, F. N. +
B. N. divided by 2. Draw a right angle line
3" long from the 11" point, and connect to the
3" width point. Draw a curve from the 2"
point down to the horizontal line. Trim out
the point. Divide the 11" line in half and
make a mark 1-3/8" in. Connect the 5"
point to the 11" point with a curve as shown in the drawing.

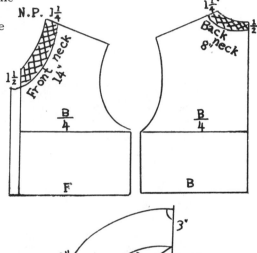

F.N. = 14"   B.N. = 8"
F.N. + B.N. ÷ 2 = 11"

7

Skirts

Straight skirts are suitable for everyone of all ages. However, if a figure has a large thigh, the skirt must be made wider at the hips. Fine woolen material, thick silk, or cotton is the best material to use for making these skirts. A regular straight skirt has a side zipper, and a kick pleat at the center back. In some straight skirts there is no kick pleat, and these must be made looser at the hips. In some skirts the back and front are joined together without a side zipper, and the zipper is put at the center back.

Drafting a Straight Skirt

Draw a right angle (⌐) line. The vertical line will be the center front, and the horizontal line will be the basic waistline. The illustration uses the medium measurements from the chart in this book.

   Waist = 28"   Hip = 38"   Skirt length = 24"

Refer to the second drawing, measure down on the center front line 24" from the right angle corner and make a mark for the skirt length. Measure down 1/2" from this right angle corner and make another mark. This 1/2" measure-ment is the formula used for making all skirts regard-less of size.

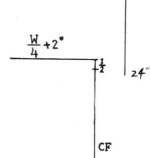

The formula to follow for marking the hip line is:

<u>8" down on center front line from the waistline</u>

Study the drawing, on the center front line measure down 8" from the waistline, and make a mark.

The formula to follow to determine the length of the hip line is:

<u>hip measurement divided by 4</u>

Using the measurements from the chart, the hip measurement equals 38" divided by 4 equals 9-1/2".

The hip line is made 8" down from the waist and 9-1/2" across.

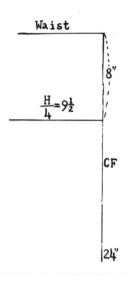

<u>Front Darts in the Skirt Front</u>

The formula for making the first dart in the skirt front is:

<u>waistline divided by 8</u>

The length of the first dart in the skirt front is:

<u>3-1/2"</u>

The formula for making the second dart in the skirt front is:

<u>1-1/2" over on the waistline from the outside line of the first dart</u>

The formula for length of the second dart in the skirt front is:

<u>2-1/2"</u>

The formula for waistline length is:

<u>waistline divided by 4 plus 2" for darts</u>

The measurements used in the drawings below are:

waistline 28" divided by 8 = 3-1/2"

waistline 28" divided by 4 = 7 + 2" for darts = 9"

darts 1" wide = 2"

Measure over on the horizontal line 3-1/2" from the right angle corner make a mark for the first dart. Make another mark over 1" for the width of the first dart. Now make a mark over 1-1/2" from this mark for the beginning of the second dart. Mark over 1" for the width of the second dart. From the outside line of the second dart measure over 2" on the horizontal line. Connect the 2" mark to the 1/2" down point on center front with a curved line. This is the waistline which should measure 9" from right angle corner including the two darts.

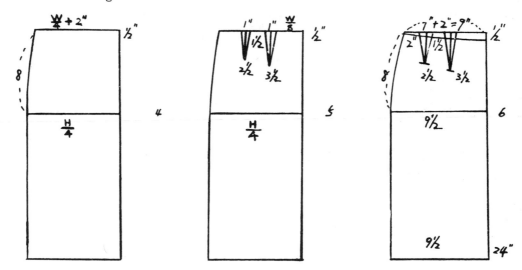

Skirt Back

The formula for the back waistline is:

down 1" from center back line

The torso drafting for the skirt back is the same except for the above formula. The darts are the same except the length of the dart differs from the length of the darts in the skirt front.

The formula for the length of the darts in the skirt back is:

first dart 4"

second dart 3-1/2"

When drafting the skirt back make a 4" extension on the center back side for the kick pleat. This extension is made parallel to the center back. On the center back line make a mark up 7" from the skirt bottom. This 7" mark is the point you stop sewing when sewing the center back seam. The center back seam is left open below this 7" mark.

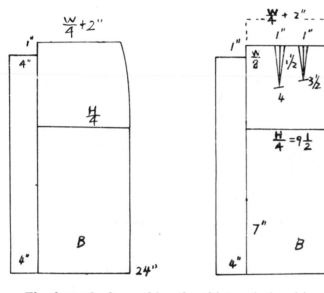

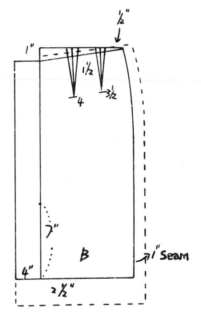

The formula for making the skirt waistband is:

width of band = 1"

length of band = 1/2 the waist measurement

When making the waistband, one end is on the fold of the material, and on the other end of the band make an extension of 1" for the lap.

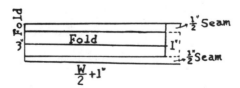

Illustration of the skirt front and back on the material.

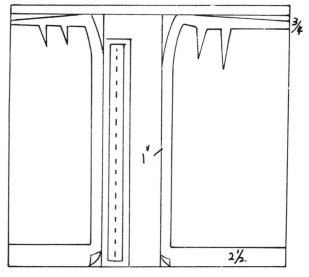

3/4" was saved at the top of the waistline for seams. 2-1/2" was saved at

the bottom for the hem, and 1" saved on the hip side.

Before cutting the skirt, check to determine if the fabric has either nap or

long hair. Velveteen, for instance, has a nap. If so, lay the skirt pattern

on the fabric in the same direction as shown in the above picture. If the fabric

has a stripe or checked pattern, adjust the design so the skirt front and the

skirt back match at the side seams. Smooth the fabric, lay pattern on and

cut.

Final Sewing of Straight Skirt

Sew the front and back waist darts.

Fold the kick pleat at the center back and sew to the 7" point.

When sewing, ease the material for the fullness at the waist.

Make the zipper opening at the left side.

Fix the belt to the waist.

Sew the hem of the skirt.

Fix the key hook, the snap, and the cord for hanging.

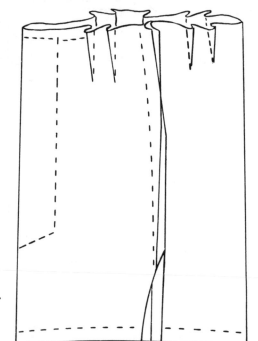

Stitch all darts.

Sew center back seam to 7" to make kick pleat.

Press darts toward side seams.

Sew up side seams. Press seams open.

Place a square of material at the 7" kick pleat point for strength. Sew across

center back at kick pleat, catching the square of material as you sew. Press

kick pleat toward the left side.

Finish seams by overcasting.

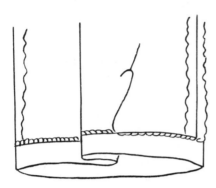

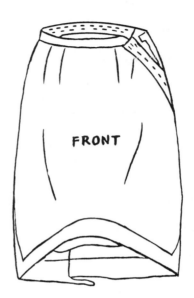

FRONT

Fold the hem of the skirt and sew.

How to fix the hook. Sew around the metal pieces with thread to attach hook and eye to the skirt band.

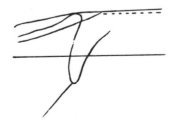

Lining a Skirt

Lay the cutout skirt on the lining material and draw around the skirt.

Do not include the hem allowance in the lining drawing.

Sew the skirt, darts, hem, and zipper in the skirt.

Sew the seams, darts, and hem in the lining.

Leave the left side of the lining open for the zipper.

Place the wrong side of the lining to the wrong side of the skirt.

Baste the lining to the skirt at the waist.

Turn under edges of lining along the zipper placket. Hand sew around the zipper to the lining.

Sew the skirtband, lining, and skirt together at the waist of the skirt.

Turn the skirtband over the lining and hand sew to the lining.

Make two chain tailor tacks 2" long on each side seam to connect the lining to the skirt at the skirt bottom.

Different Style Skirts

Drape the cloth over a dress form or chair, and study the cloth to determine which style skirt you wish to make.

Gathered Skirt

In a gathered skirt the lines are soft and irregular.

The formula for figuring the amount of material necessary for a gathered skirt is:

<u>Waist measurement times 3</u>

<u>Method of Sewing Gathered Skirt</u>

At the top of the material (be sure selvedge of the material is on each side) sew two rows with a loose stitch. Pull the threads to make the material the size of the waist measurement. Sew up one side leaving 8'' opening for zipper. Sew a 3'' hem at the bottom. This 3'' hem is always necessary for a gathered skirt.

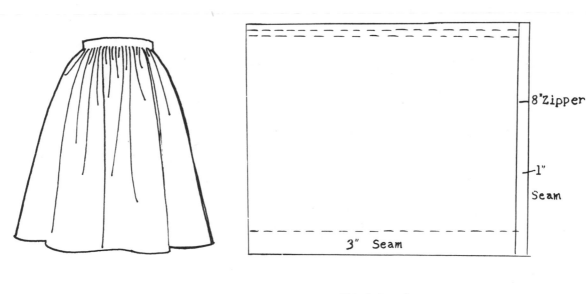

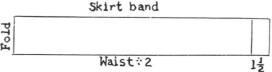

Pleated Skirt

The lines in a pleated skirt are hard and clear.

The formula to follow for figuring the amount of material to buy for a pleated

skirt is:

Waist measurement times 3

The formula for figuring pleats is:

Amount of material necessary (as figured above) minus waist

measurement = amount left for pleats

It is always necessary to have 16 pleats in the skirt.

The formula for figuring the width of the outside pleat is:

Waist measurement divided by 16

The formula for figuring the width of the inside pleat is:

Amount of material left for pleats divided by 16

The measurements used in the drawing were taken from the chart of

average measurements on page 15.   Using the above formulas and these

measurements, study the equations below so you will understand how to

make a pleated skirt for your measurements.

Waist = 28",   28" times 3 = 84" (amount of material necessary)

84" minus 28" (waist measurement) - 56" (left for pleats)

56" divided by 16 = 3-1/2" for width of inside pleat

28" (waist measurement) divided by 16 pleats = 1-3/4" for width of outside pleat.

The drawing is half of the total skirt.   Waist is 28", hip is 38", skirt length

is 24".   Material is 84", fold is 42".   At zipper opening (either on the

side or back) make half of the pleat on each side of the zipper.

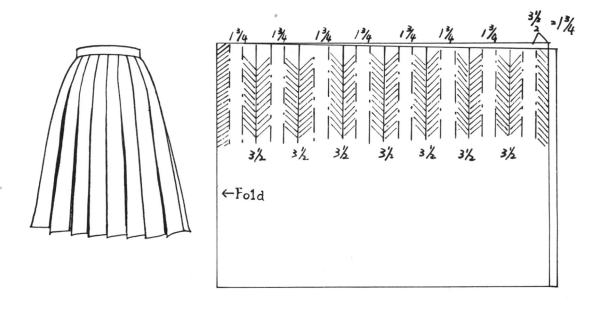

1¾ 1¾ 1¾ 1¾ 1¾ 1¾ 1¾ 3½ =1¾

3½ 3½ 3½ 3½ 3½ 3½ 3½

←Fold

Culottes

Culottes are very much like a skirt. Follow the principles for drawing any skirt, and make the necessary changes below the hip line. Draw the hip line and waistline darts. Measure down from the waistline the amount equal to the crotch length plus 1/2 inch. The front crotch extension uses the hip measurement divided by 12. The back crotch uses the hip measurement divided by 8. The back waistline is drawn down 1/4" and is drawn in 3/4" from the center back line. To make a center pleat, add 4" to the center front line as illustrated.

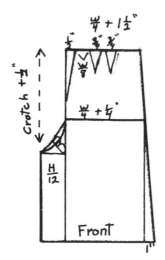

$\frac{H}{4} + 1\frac{1}{2}"$

Crotch $+\frac{1}{2}"$

$\frac{H}{8}$

$\frac{H}{4} + \frac{1}{4}"$

$\frac{H}{12}$

Front

1"

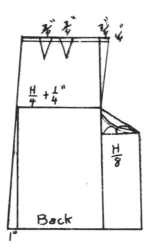

$\frac{H}{4} + \frac{1}{4}"$

$\frac{H}{8}$

Back

1"

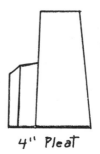

4" Pleat

This skirt has big waves downward, and a gentle sloping line.

Fold the material in a square first, then fold again into a triangle.

Move down from the point of the triangle until you are able to measure the amount figured in the formula across the pattern.

The formula for drafting a circle skirt is:

Waist measurement divided by 6 = amount to measure across

the pattern

In our drawing the waist measurement is 28" divided by 6 = 4-5/8". Move down from the triangle point until you can make a line across the pattern equal to 7". Draw a line with a curved ruler. This is the waistline. Measure down from the waistline for the skirt length and make a mark. Measure from waistline down the skirt measurement in several places so hem will be even. Always make the hem in a circle skirt 1-1/2" wide.

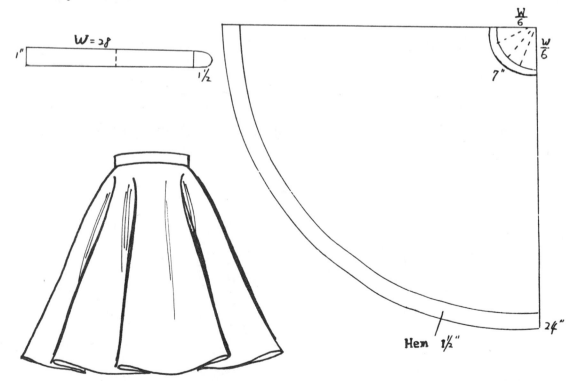

Skirt with Center Front Pleat

Follow the directions for the straight skirt. Draw
a straight skirt on the material. Add 5" across and
down the center front. When sewing this skirt, this
center front seam will be sewn 7" down from the
skirt top; so make a mark 7" down from the
skirt top. The skirt will be open from the 7" point to the skirt
bottom. Extend the skirt bottom 1" on hip side.
Connect the 1" extension to the hip line with a straight
line.

The formula to follow for the position of the first dart
in a skirt with one dart is:

<u>Waist measurement divided by 8</u>

Using the average waist measurement 28" divided by 8 =
3-1/2". Measure over 3-1/2" from center front and make
the dart 1" wide and 4" long. The formula to
follow to determine the skirt waist length is:

<u>Waist measurement divided by 4 + 1"</u>

28" divided by 4 = 7" + 1" = 8".

Draw in waistline length 8" across the
waistline from the center front line.

Back

Follow the same directions to make the back
as you did for the skirt front, except the back dart is 1-1/2" wide.

Band

Length of skirtband is waist measurement plus 1-1/2". Make the band 3" wide
and finished band will be 1".

Draw a straight skirt following the procedure at the beginning of this chapter.

Extend the skirt bottom 1-1/2" on the hip side.

Measure up 1/2". Connect the 1/2" point to the hip line with a straight line.

Back

Draw the back following the same directions followed for the skirt front.

Skirt Band

The length of the skirt band is determined by the waist measurement plus 1-1/2". The band should be made 3" wide and finished will be 1" wide.

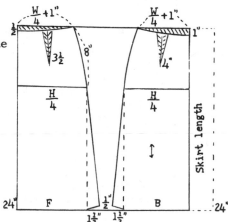

Faced Skirt

This skirt can be faced rather than belted. Cut a band 1-1/2" wide and the length of the waist measurement. With right sides together sew facing to skirt, turn to wrong side, press, stitch 1/2 inch down in each dart to hold facing down.

Turn in seam allowance on the bottom of the facing edge.

Flare Skirt

Follow the directions for making the straight
skirt. Draw a straight skirt on the material.
Extend the center front line 1-1/2". Measure
up 1/2" from the skirt bottom. Connect this
point with a straight line to the hip line.
Extend the skirt bottom on the hip side 2-1/2".
Measure up 1" on the hip side and connect the
1" point to the hip line with a straight line.
The dart in this skirt is figured the same way
as the dart in the skirt with a center front pleat.

Back

Follow the same directions used for the skirt
front. Study the drawing.

Band

The length of the skirtband is determined by
the waist measurement plus 1-1/2" and is cut 3" wide.

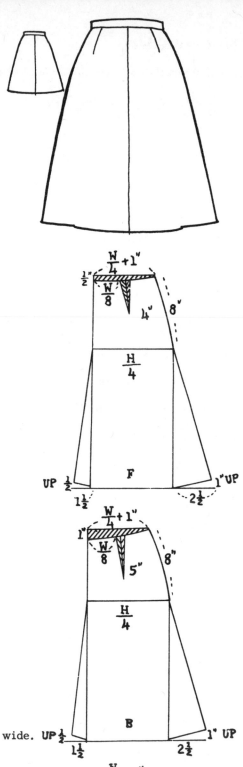

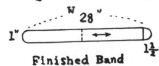

Finished Band

Six Gore Skirt

Always make this skirt in paper first before cutting the fabric. Never mark the fabric and cut this style skirt. Draw a straight skirt following the directions on page 69. Draw the first dart and extend the dart to the skirt length line. Cut on this line from the bottom of the dart to the skirt length line. At the top of the skirt cut on both dart lines. The front panel is the section which is on the fold. The other section is called the hip section. When cutting the skirt cut one front panel and two hip sections. Follow the same procedure for drawing the skirt back.

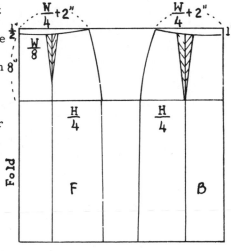

To make the skirt flare, extend the skirt length line 1" on each side of the cut line and connect with a straight line to the hip line. To make the skirt hang evenly, it is necessary to measure up 1/4" from the bottom of the skirt on the hip side and connect the 1/4" point with a straight line to the hip line. Note the drawing that a 1" extension is added to the skirt bottom on the hip side as well as on each side of the cut line.

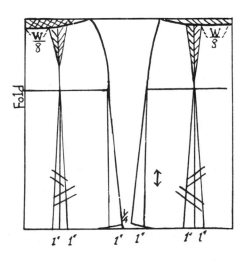

Six Gore Skirt Finished Drawing

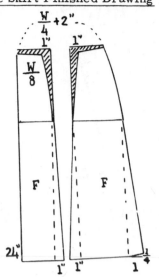

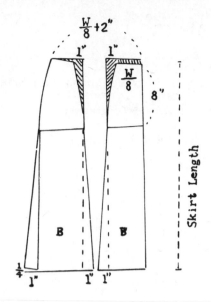

If desired, the skirt may be hand-stitched with embroidery thread along the gores as shown in the picture.

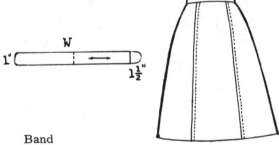

Band

Draw the skirtband the length equal to the waist measurement. Extend the line 1-1/2" for the button and buttonhole. Draw the band 3" wide to make a 1" finished band.

8

Blouses

Blouses

When making an overblouse, 4" must be added to the bottom of the front and back torso. When making a tuck-in blouse, 6" must be added to the torso front and back. The formula to follow for figuring the blouse opening down the center front or back is:

Save 3" (2" to fold under and 1" for the buttons).

If the opening is down the center back, it is necessary to save this 3" on both backs; if the opening is down the center front, save 3" on both fronts. In drafting a pattern for a blouse, use the regular front and back torso.

Blouse with Peter Pan Collar

The opening in this blouse is down the center front. Using the regular front torso, save 3" mentioned. above. Mark over 1/2" on the shoulder line and mark down 1" on the center front line. Connect these two points with a curved ruler. Trim out the extra taken off the torso by drawing these new lines.

Dart

Draw an underarm dart down 4"

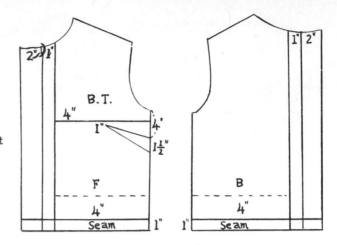

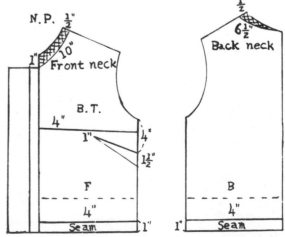

from the underarm. Connect to the bust tip. Measure down 1" from the bust tip and complete the dart making it 1-1/2" wide.

Note: The bust dart is drawn in this manner for all blouses in this chapter.

Back

Use the regular back torso, mark over 1/2" on the shoulder line from the neck point and connect to the center back line.

Peter Pan Collar

The formula for figuring the length of the collar is:

Front neck measurement plus back neck measurement

divided by 2

Measure to the end of the 1" lap on the front torso for correct front neck length. Using the figures in the chart on page 15: front neck = 10" + back neck 6-1/2" divided by 2 = 8-1/4".

Draw a right angle (⌐). Measure 5" up on this line and make a mark, add 2" to this line. Connect the 5" point with a straight line to the left end of the length line 8-1/4" long. The formula for drawing the neck curve is:

Divide the straight line in half from the 5" point to the length

line and make a mark out 1-1/2" at this half point

Follow the above formula, draw a curved line from the 5" point, touch the 1-1/2" mark, connect to the length line. At the left end of the length line draw a 2" right angle line. Be sure to measure from the neck curve out 2" at several points so the collar will be 2" wide the entire length of the collar. Connect with a curved line to the 2" point on the right side. At the corner point of the right angle line measure in 1/2" and make a curve to round the collar.

As stated in the title, this blouse is made with a straight yoke across the back and is made in striped fabric. The stripes running in different directions give this blouse an interesting effect. To draw this blouse, draw a regular front torso. Since the style is open down the front, add 3" on both sides of the center front as done in previous blouses of the same style.

Back

Draw a regular back torso. Measure down the center back 5" from the neck, and draw a straight line across the torso from the center back to the armhole. This line will be the same as the back width line on the regular back torso. Cut the torso on this line and lay on the fabric, add 1" for seams and cut. When laying the torso on the material, place the torso so the stripe of the fabric will run across the torso from armhole to armhole. The remaining part of the back torso is placed on the fabric so the stripe will run up and down. Add 1" for seams to the back width line, which is the top of the torso where the yoke was cut, and finish cutting the back torso. This same style may be used for a dress with a cut waist using any of the style skirts shown in this book.

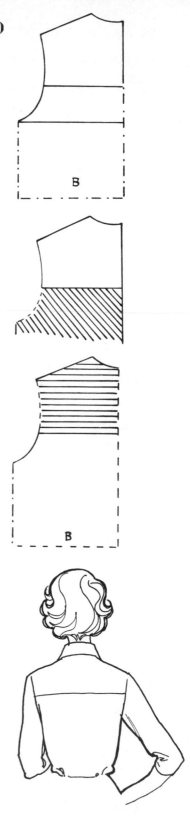

Blouse with Pointed Back Yoke Style

Draw a back torso, copy back width line down 5",
and bust line from the original back torso.
Divide the area on the center back from neck to
the bust line into three equal parts. Draw a
straight line from armhole edge of the back width
line to the second division point on the center
back. Add 1" seams before cutting.

To finish the back, use the remaining back torso
adding 1" for seams on the cut line and cut.
Use the regular front torso adding 3" down the
center front for front opening to finish the blouse.
This style may also be used for a dress with a cut
waistline.

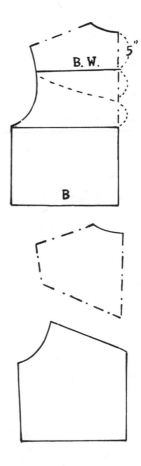

Blouse with a Back Scallop Yoke Style

Draw a back torso. Copy the back width
and bust lines from the original torso.
Divide the back width line into three equal parts.
To draw the first scallop, make a mark from
armhole edge to the first division and down 1".
Connect from armhole edge with a curved line
to the second division. To draw the second
scallop, make a mark on the center back down
1" and connect with a curved line to the second division.
Cut the torso on the scallop lines, place on the material
and add 1/2" for seams before cutting. The bottom of the
back torso or the section remaining is cut straight across
on the back width line. Place on the material, add 1" for
seams on the back width line and cut. This style blouse
may be used as a dress with any style skirt.

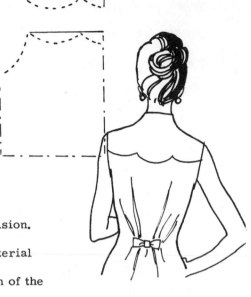

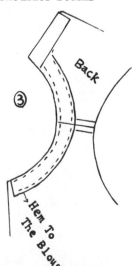

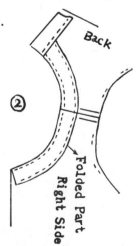

Facings for Collarless, Sleeveless Blouse

To cut the facing for the neck of a collarless blouse, pin the shoulder seams
of the front and back torsos together.

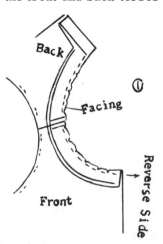

Back

Facing ①

Front

Reverse Side

Back ②

Folded Part Right Side

Back ③

Hem To The Blouse

Place the torso on another piece of paper and draw around the neck. Remove
the torso and measure 2" out from line just drawn all around the neck making
the facing 2" wide.

Facing for the sleeveless blouse is made by pinning the shoulder seams,
drawing around the armhole, removing the torso and making the facing 2"
out from the line all around as done for the collar above.

All of the torsos given for these blouses have been for sleeveless styles.
To draft a torso for blouses with sleeves, add 2-1/2" to the armhole of
the original torsos. The armhole measurement from the chart on page 15
is 16"+ 2-1/2" = 18-1/2".

18-1/2" divided by 2 = 9-1/4".

Measure from the shoulder around the armhole 9-1/4", connect this measurement to the underarm bust line.

When cutting this torso save 1/2" for seams all around the armhole.

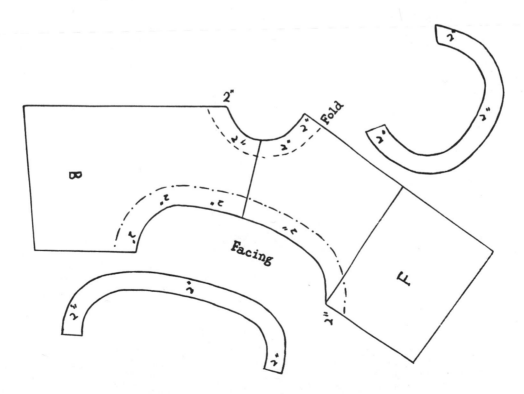

Blouse with Boat Neck Style

Draw a front torso. Measure over on the shoulder line 3" from the center front neck and make a mark. Extend the center front line at the neck 1/2". At the armhole edge of the shoulder line make a mark down 1/2". Connect the 3" mark on the shoulder to the 1/2" extension on the center front with a straight line. Connect the 3" mark on the shoulder to the 1/2" down point at the armhole edge. Trim away the extra torso used to draft the boat neck.

 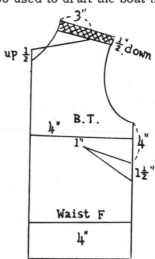

Draw a back torso. Make a mark 3" over on the shoulder line from the center back neck. Make a mark down 1/2" on center back. Connect this point with a curved line to the 3" point on the shoulder. Extend the shoulder line at the armhole edge 1/2", and connect 3" point on the shoulder line with a straight line.

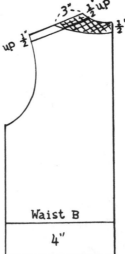

Blouse with Rolled Collar

The opening for this style blouse is in the back.

Use the regular front torso. On front torso mark over 1" from the neck point on the shoulder line, and mark down 1" on the center front line from the neck. Connect with a curved line.

Use the regular back torso and add 3" at the center back (2" for fold under and 1" for buttons). Mark over 1" on shoulder from the neck point and connect to the center back with a curved line.

Rolled Collar

Use the previously given formula to determine collar length (F.N.+B.N. divided by 2) 10-1/2" +7" divided by 2=8-3/4".

Draw a line 8-3/4" long. Draw another line up 8" on the right side, across 8-3/4", and down 8" forming a square. Divide this 8" line in half, and draw a line across the collar at this point extending the line 3/4" at the left side. Connect this extension with a straight line to the top and bottom corner of the square. This creates a point on the end of the collar. This collar must be cut on the bias of the material.

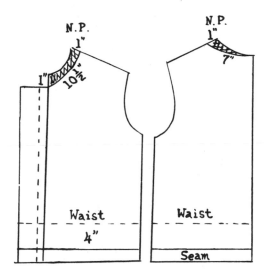

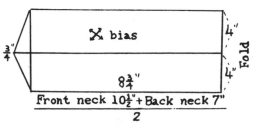

Blouse with V Neck and Ruffle Collar

This style blouse has a front opening. Use regular front torso with 3" saved at center front as in previous drawings. Measure down 4" at center front and over 1" on shoulder line. Using a straight ruler connect 4" point to 1" point with a straight line.

Use the regular back torso, and mark over 1" at shoulder line. Connect the new shoulder mark to the center back with a curved line.

Ruffle

Use the selvedge of the fabric for the outside of the ruffle.

Measure around the neck (across the back) and down the front to the waist. Multiply this measurement by 2. Draw a line the length of this measurement. Add a 2" line to this line, draw across the length of the other line and down 2" forming a square. Using the measure-

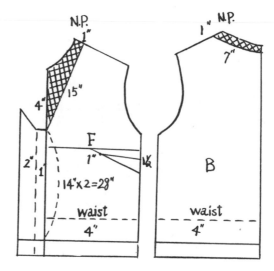

ments from the drawing 15" + 14 + 7" = 36" times 2 (because this measurement is for only one side) = 72".

72" times 3 determines the amount of fabric for the ruffle. 72" x 3 = 216".

The drawing below shows the material folded. It is 108" long.

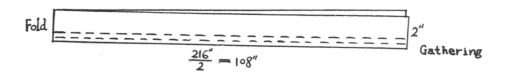

Circle Ruffle

Either the straight ruffle just described or the circle ruffle can be used on this style blouse. The circle ruffle is 3" wide. Draw a circle which measures 1" in diameter from the center at all points of the circle. Draw extension lines in four different parts from this circle 3" wide. Connect these extension lines to form another circle outside the original circle. Cut in on one of the extension lines to the small circle. Cut around the small circle. Measure around this small circle. Measure the entire neck plus down the front to the waist of the blouse to determine how many circles to cut to fit the neck and blouse front to the waist. It usually requires 7 circles. Sew the circles together to finish ruffle on the blouse.

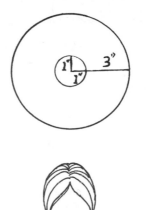

Blouse with Tie Collar

This style has a front opening. Use the regular front torso, and follow the directions for the 3" saved at center front. At the center front make a mark down 1" from the neck and over 1/2" from the neck point on the shoulder line. Connect these points as done in previous drawings with a curve.

Use the regular back torso and mark down

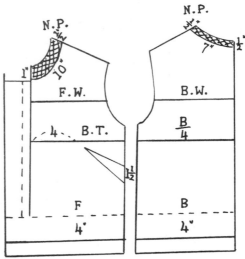

1/2" on center back from neck, and over from neck point on shoulder line 1/2". Connect these two points with a curved line.

Tie Collar

Measure around the neck of the torso. Back and front neck measurements divided by two equals the length to make the collar. Using the measurements from the chart F. N. = 10" + B. N. 7" divided by 2 = 8-1/2".

Draw a line 8-1/2" long. Draw a straight line at the right of this line 2-1/2" long. Connect the 2-1/2" mark to the left end of the 8-1/2" line with a straight line. Divide this line in half, extend half mark 3/4". Draw a curved line from the 2-1/2" point, touch 3/4" point, and connect to the 8-1/2" point. At the left corner make a line up 3", connect to the 4" wide point with a curved ruler.

At the left length line, extend the line 8" (make this line longer if a long tie is desired, but do not make any shorter than 8"). Make this extension 3" wide. Connect to the top of the existing collar. The collar ends may be designed in any desired style.

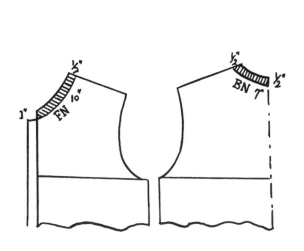

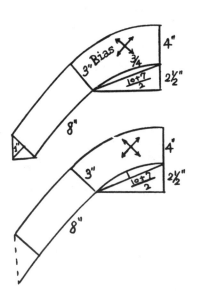

Center front opening is used for this style blouse. Use the regular front and back torso drawing. Save 5" at the center front as previously explained. Use the original front and back torso and make no changes.

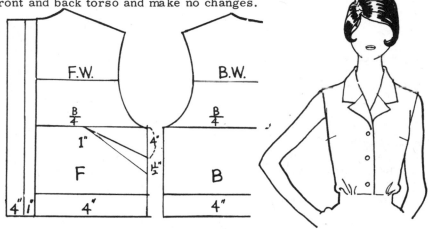

Shirt Collar

To determine the length of the shirt collar follow the formula:

Neck measurement divided by 2

Using the measurement from the chart, neck measurement = 14-1/2" divided by 2=7-1/4" draw a straight line 7-1/4" long. Add a right angle line to the right end of this line 2-1/2" long. Draw a line across and down to the left end the length line forming a square. Extend the top line on the left 3/4". Measure up 1/2" and make a mark. Connect this mark to the 3/4" extension line with a straight line. Divide the neck length line into three equal parts. Connect the 1/2" point to the first division on the neck length line.

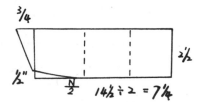

Blouse with a Sailor Collar

Draw a front torso. On center front, measure from bust line up 3/4". From the neck point measure over on the shoulder line 1/2", connect these two lines.

<u>Back</u>

Draw a back torso. Measure down 1/4" on center back from the neck. Measure from neck point over on shoulder line 1/2", connect these two lines. Trim out extra.

<u>Making the Collar</u>

Place the back torso on the front torso so back shoulder line is 1-1/2" over front torso at armhole edge. On front torso, measure over from the bottom of the V at the neck 1". On the back torso measure from the neck down the center back 6". Draw a straight line across the back to the arm-

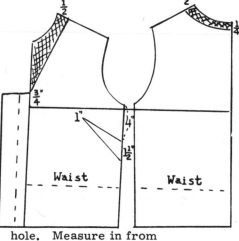

hole. Measure in from the armhole edge 3/4". Connect the 3/4" to the 1" front neck point with a straight line. Cut out the collar on the completed collar lines. Study the drawing carefully as the directions are read.

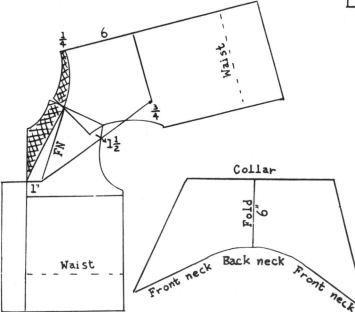

Sailor Collar

Chinese Mandarin Collar Blouse with Cap Sleeve

Draw the regular front torso. For this blouse save 3" down the center front (2" for fold under and 1" for buttons).

Back

Draw the regular back torso, and make no changes for this style blouse.

Cap Sleeve

Refer to drawing on this page, at armhole edge measure down 1/4", connect to the shoulder. This 1/4" measurement is made to prevent the shoulder line from sticking out.

Mandarin Collar

Draw a right angle (⌐). Measure up 1-1/4" from the right angle corner. Follow formula neck measurement divided by 2. Using the chart figures 14-1/2" ÷ 2 = 7-1/4". Measure over from the right angle corner 7-1/4", and make a mark. Measure up 1-1/4" at the 7-1/4" point, and draw a line across to the other 1-1/4" point. On the left corner of the square extend the line up 1-1/4". Divide the 7-1/4" length line in half, and draw a line from this half point to connect to the beginning of the 1-1/4" extension.

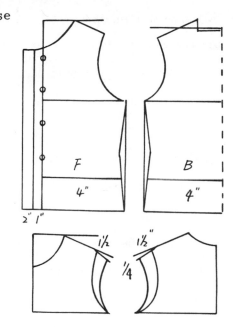

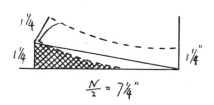

Cowl Neck Blouse

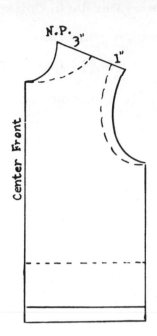

Draw this torso on paper first, then lay the torso on the bias fold of the material before cutting. Draw a front torso. Measure over 3" from the neck point on the shoulder line, connect this measurement with a curved line to the center front neck. Extend the shoulder line 1" at the armhole edge, connect the extension to the armhole. Divide the line from the neck point to the shoulder point into two parts. Measure down the center front from the neck 3", draw a curved line to the new neck point (3" point across the shoulder line). Draw another line 1" down the center front from the 3" line and connect to the half division on the shoulder line.

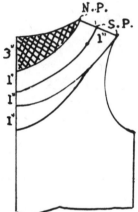

Draw a third line down 1" from the last line and connect this line to the shoulder point. Cut along all three lines stopping 1" before the shoulder line. Cut out the torso drawing.

Fold the fabric on the bias ( ). Place the paper pattern, which has been folded down the center front, on the fabric so the center front is on the fold of the fabric. Raise each cutout section 1" (the paper cutout sections will extend over the fold of the material when they

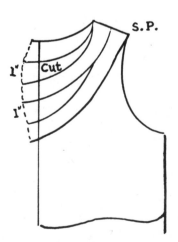

are raised 1"). Draw around the neck, shoulder, armhole, down the side, and across the bottom. Cut out.

Back

Draw a back torso. Measure over from the neck point on the shoulder line 3", connect with a curved line to the neck at the center back. <u>Do not cut the back of this blouse on the bias of the material.</u>

Extend the shoulder line 1" at the armhole edge, connect the extension to the armhole the same as for the front torso.

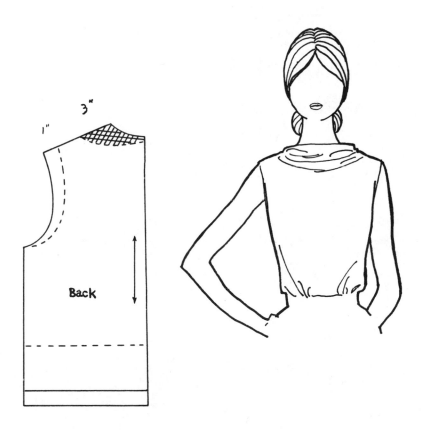

9

Pants, Slacks & Shorts

Slacks

The formulas for drafting slacks front

are:

(1) figuring the width of the crotch:

hip measurement divided by 4 + 1"

(2) figuring the length of the crotch:

hip measurement divided by 4 + 1-1/2"

Using the above formulas and the hip measurement

from the chart on page 15, study the formulas

below:

38" divided by 4=9-1/2" + 1" = 10-1/2"

38" divided by 4=9-1/2" + 1-1/2" = 11"

Draw a vertical line 38" long. Follow the above

formula for figuring the length of the crotch.

Measure down 11" from the top line. This is the

length of the crotch.

Following the formula above to determine the width

of the crotch, (hip measurement 38" divided by 4+1"

= 10-1/2"). Draw a line down 11" and across 10-1/2".

$\frac{4}{4} + 1" = 10\frac{1}{2}"$ 11"

38"

The formula to follow for making the slacks crotch is:

<u>measure in 2" on crotch side</u>

On the crotch side of the 10-1/2" line measure in 2".

Measure up 3-1/2" from the 2" mark on the crotch

line. From this 10-1/2" mark draw a straight line

up 11". Draw a straight line from the 2" point up 11"

long connecting the two 11" lines and forming a square.

Draw a straight line connecting the 2" point with the

3-1/2" point. Divide this line in half and at this half

point draw a line in 1/2". Curve a line from the 2"

point. Touch the 1/2" point, and continue to the 3-1/2"

point.

Follow the second illustration on this page, divide

the 10-1/2" + 2" = 12-1/2" line in half (6-1/4").

Measure across the 12-1/2" line from the hip side

6-1/4". At this 6-1/4" point draw one long line from

the slacks waist down to the 38" length position.

This is the slacks crease line. At the 38" length

position, measure over 3" on each side of the 6-1/4"

line. Draw a line across connecting these points

making the slacks length line. Connect the 3" point

on the hip side to the 6-1/4" point on the crotch line.

Divide the 2" line at the crotch in half. Connect this

1/2" point to the 3" point at the slacks length.

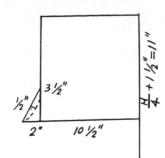

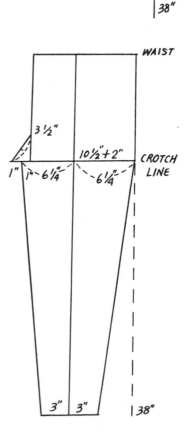

Slacks Front

Divide the crease line from the crotch to the slacks length in half. Measure up 1/2" from this half point, and draw a line across the slacks. Divide the area from this new line to crotch line in half. Use a curved ruler (curve inward) to connect the 2" extension at the crotch to this half point.

Darts in the Slacks

The first dart is marked on the crease line 5" down and 1/2" each side of the crease line or 1" for the entire width of the dart.

The second dart is made by making a mark over 1-1/2" from the outside first dart line. Measure over from this line 1", make a mark, mark the dart 3" long. Connect these dart width marks to the dart length mark with straight lines to form the dart.

Waist

Or the crotch side at the waistline measure in 1/4". Use the formula, waistline divided by 4 + 2" to determine the waistline length. Using the chart measurements, waistline = 28" divided by 4 + 2" = 9". Measure over 9" on the waistline from the 1/4" in point. At the crotch line measure in 1", connect this 1" point to the 9" waistline with a curved ruler (curve outward) to the crotch line. A straight line connects the crotch line to the bottom of the slacks.

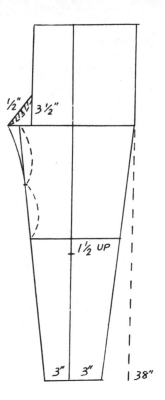

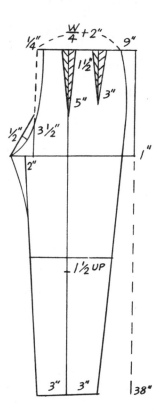

Flare Leg Pants

Slacks Back

Lay the front slacks on the fabric. Make the following changes by following the dotted lines in the drawing:

On the crotch side of the waistline, measure over 1-1/2" and draw a line up 1". Draw a straight line across from the 1" point 9" long. Connect the 1-1/2" point to the crotch with a curved line. On the crotch line at the crotch extend the line 2", measure down 3/8", and connect with a curved line to the crotch curve as shown in the drawing. Add 1/2" along both sides of the slacks leg.

Cutting the Slacks

Add 1/2" seams at the waistline, and on both sides. Also add 1-1/2" at the bottom before cutting for the hem. The two drawings show front and back slacks.

Flare Leg Pants

To draw the flare leg pants extend the line at the slacks front and back out 2" (or whatever amount to achieve the flare desired) on inside and outside of the leg. Connect this line to a point at midcalf or wherever you want the flare to start.

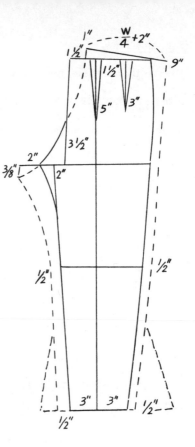

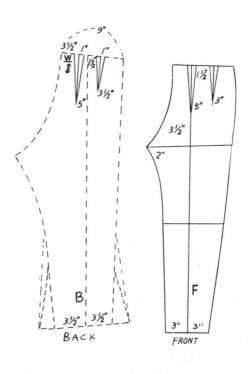

Follow the same drawing as for the slacks front except the first dart is down 6" instead of 5". Add 1/2" seam at both sides and waistline and add 1-1/2" at the bottom before cutting. Always make a 1-1/2" hem in slacks and shorts.

<u>Back</u>

To draw shorts back, draw the front and extend the back by following the dotted lines in the picture below.

Extend the crotch 2" and measure down 1/2" from crotch line, connect with a curved line.

Bermuda Shorts

Bermuda shorts length is 2" above the knee, but it can be shorter if desired. Pedal pushers are made the same way but the length covers the knee.

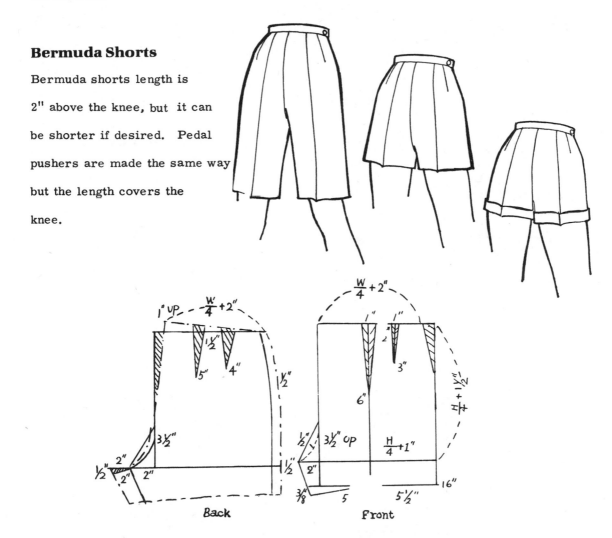

Back   Front

The illustrations below show short shorts, Bermuda shorts, and slacks.

Notice the darts and waistline are the same for all three articles except

the length is different.

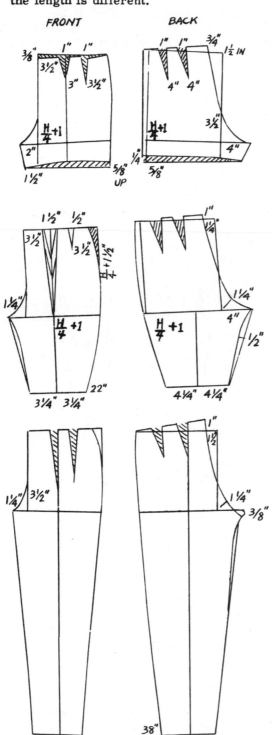

Hot Pants

Hot pants are really only short shorts with or without a cuff. Make them the same way as the Bermuda shorts, only make them as short as desired. Remember to allow some length for sitting because when you sit the shorts will draw up shorter.

Cuff

Cut a 4" band the length of the hot pants bottom. Fold in half, stitch to bottom of hot pants with raw edges inside. Turn cuff to outside or right side.

Bib

Some hot pants have a bib attached. To make the bib, cut two squares of fabric the desired length from waist to underarm plus seam allowance. With right sides together sew around the top and two sides -- turn, press, top stitch. Add straps, cut 3" wide. Sew as a belt, turn, press, and attach to front with buttons and buttonholes. Cross the straps in the back and sew to pants back.

Pants Suits

Make flare pants and any of the blouses, dresses, or suit coats illustrated in this book. Blouses and dresses used in pants suits can be made longer by lowering the length of the featured garments.

10

Dresses

Simple Dresses

The following measurements from the average chart on page 15 will be used to demonstrate the drafting of these simple dresses:

Dress length	40"	Bust	36"
Hip	38"	Waist	28"
Front width	14"	Back width	14-1/2"
Shoulder	15-1/2"	Back waist length	16"
Front waist length	17-1/2"		

Shift Dress

Draw the front torso. Extend the center front line down the length of the dress or in this drawing 40".

The formula to determine the bust point is:

measure down 10" on center front from neck and across 4"

from the center front

Using the above formula make a mark for the bust point. Draw a straight line from the waist to the bust point.

The formula to determine the width of the bust dart is:

front waist length measurment - back waist length measurement

Using the above formula, the front waist length measurement in our drawing is 17-1/2" minus the back waist length 16" equals 1-1/2". So the bust dart is drawn 1-1/2" wide. Return to your drawing and make a mark up 1-1/2" from the waist on the side edge, connect this mark with a straight line to the bust point to finish the bust dart.

The formula to determine the length of the waistline:

Waistline measurement divided by 4 + 1"

Following the above formula and the measurements given, 28" divided by 4 + 1" = 8". Measure across from center front on waistline 8" and make a mark. Connect from underarm to this waist point with a curved ruler (curve inward). The formula to determine the length of the hip line across the torso: Hip measurement divided by 4.

Using the measurements from the chart and the above formula:

38" divided by 4 = 9-1/2"

To draw the hip line on our pattern, measure down 8" from the waistline and draw a line across 9-1/2". The position for the hip line is 8" down for everyone. Use a curved ruler with the curve of the ruler turned outward, and connect the waistline to the 8" hip line. Connect the hip line to the dress length line with a straight line. The formula to determine the position of the waist dart is:

measure from the hip line up 2"

measure from the bust point down 2"

dart is 1" wide.

Draw the back torso by laying the front torso on the fabric and tracing around it. Be sure to fold and pin the bust dart on the lines drawn. Add a 1" seam all along center back for the zipper. Use a 22" zipper. Make a mark down the center back from top of neck down 22" to indicate the end of the zipper. Save 1" seams at the shoulder, sides of dress, and 1/2" around armhole edge and 3" at the bottom for the hem.

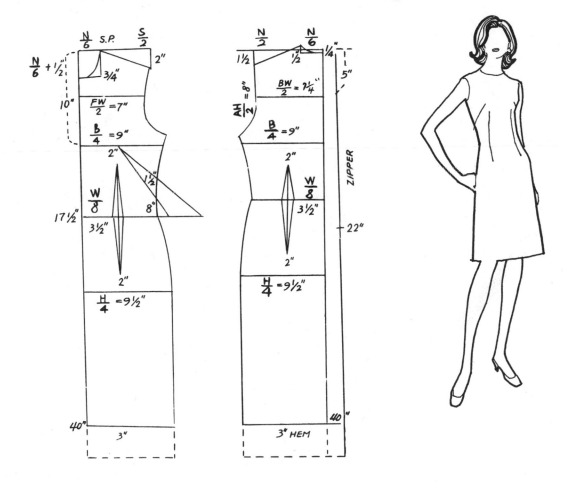

V Neck A-Line Shift Dress

Draw a front torso putting in darts, and follow the same directions used for the shift dress. The formula for determining the length of the A-line is:

hip measurement divided by 4 + 1/4"

Using the 38" hip measurement, 38" divided by 4 + 1/4" = 9-3/4". Measure from the center front across 9-3/4", connect this point to the hip line with a curved line and to the hem line.

To Draft the V Neck

Measure down from the center front neck 4". Measure over on the shoulder line 1", connect these two marks with a straight ruler.

Back

Draw a back torso, measure from neck point over on shoulder line 1", measure from neck down center back 1/2". Connect these two measurements with a curved line. Add 1" seam allowance down the center back for zipper, and make a mark down from the center back 22" to indicate the position to sew the zipper. The A-Line dress may be made looser for comfort. Add 1/4" to each measurement for this looser style.

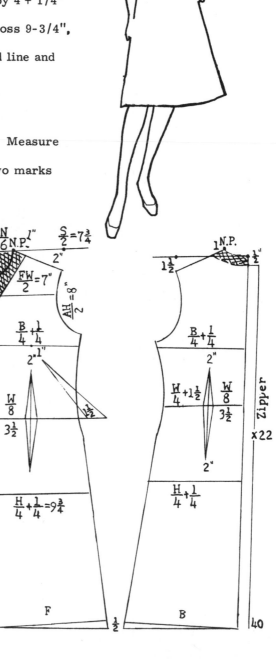

Following the measurements from the chart on page 15, make the following

changes to achieve this looser style:

F.W. divided by 2 = 7" (14" divided by 2 = 7")

B. divided by 4 + 1/4" = 9-1/4" (36" divided by 4+1/4"= 9-1/4")

W. divided by 4 + 2" + 1" = 9-1/2" (28" divided by 4 + 2" + 1" = 9-1/2")

H. divided by 4 + 1/4" = 9-3/4"

Empire Dress

The front waistline darts are lengthened on the diagram of this

empire A-Line style dress. If no seam is desired at the armhole,

fold the dart before cutting. The skirt has been A-lined 1".

This style can be used as an evening dress by lengthening the skirt.

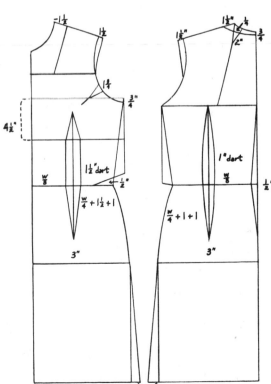

Draw a front torso, extend the center front line 40" for the dress length.
Measure over on the shoulder line 3" from the neck point on front torso and
make a mark. Extend the center front line 1/2". At shoulder point measure down 1/2" and make a mark. Connect these two marks with a straight
line. Connect the 3" over mark on the shoulder line to 1/2" extension on
center front. Trim away the extra torso used to draft the boat neck. Follow previous directions and mark in darts, bust line, waistline measurement and hip line.

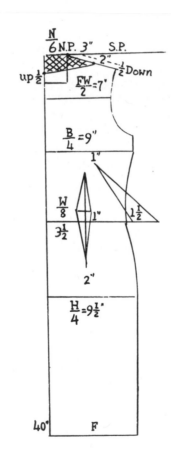

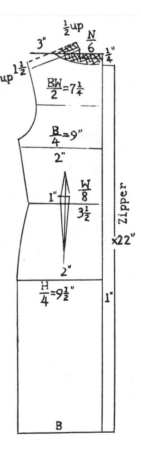

Simple Shift Dress with Gathered Effect at Waist

This style dress may be made with a casing at the waist with a belt through it, or elastic may be put in the casing instead of a belt. Draw a shift dress torso. Draw a straight line from armhole down to the length line of the dress. Do not have any shaping at the waist. Sew a strip of material 1" wide cut on the selvedge edge at the waist. Measure from the neck point to the waist plus 1" and sew casing in this position. Insert elastic or a belt through the casing. If a belt is used, make a buttonhole on each side of the center front so belt can be tied in front of dress. An inch has been added down the center back for buttons.

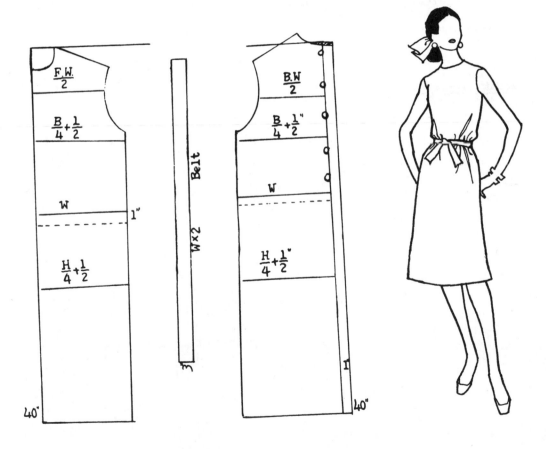

Simple Dress with Cut Waistline

Draw a front torso. Copy the front width line and bust line from the original torso. Draw the bust dart following the same procedure followed when drawing the shift dress.

The formula to determine the position of the first waistline dart is:

waistline measurement divided by 8

Using the measurements from the chart, study the following equation:

28" divided by 8 = 3-1/2"

Measure from the center front line across 3-1/2" on waistline and make a mark for the first dart. Make another mark 1/2" from this mark and another mark 1/2" further on. On the second mark draw a straight line up to a point 2" below the bust point. Finish making dart by connecting the 1/2" marks on the waistline to the top of the dart line 2" down from bust point.

The formula for determining the waist length measurement is:

waistline measurement divided by 4 + 1" (dart)

Using the above formula and the measurements in the drawing, 28" divided by 4 + 1" = 8". Make a mark 8" from the center front across the waistline. Fold the bust dart on the dart lines and connect the waistline point with a curved ruler (curve inward) to the armhole.

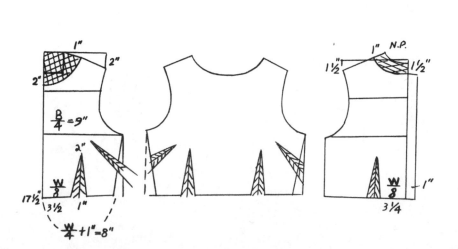

Save 1" at the shoulders, sides and waistline bottom for seams and 1/2" around the armhole edge. Any style neckline may be used with this style dress. Refer to Chapter 8.

Skirt for Simple Cut Waistline Style Dress

Draw a straight skirt from the directions given in this book for straight skirts. Be sure waistline darts in waist front and back match the darts in skirt front and back. To draft different style necklines on simple shift dresses follow neckline directions in Chapter 8.

Belt

The formula to follow for making a simple tie belt for any of these dresses is:

waist measurement times 2

width of the belt 3" (finished 1")

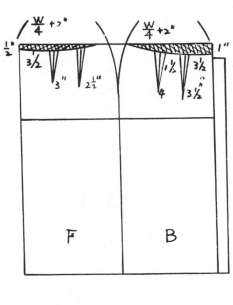

Simple Dress with Gathered Skirt

To draw the waist for this style dress, follow the original front and back torso and add 1" all around the torso for seams.

To cut the skirt, use two widths of the material and the skirt length measurement. Sew the widths together on the selvedge of the material and gather the top to fit the waist measurement.

All of these style dresses are sleeveless. Make the armhole adjustments on the front and back torso if sleeves are desired. Consult Chapter 8 for armhole adjustments.

Draw a front torso. The formula to follow for the front width line is:

>   front width measurement divided by 2 (14" divided by 2=7")

Draw the front width line down 3" from neck point and across 7". To draw the

neck, measure from the neck point across the shoulder line 2". Make a strap

1" over from the 2" point. Draw the strap straight down to the front width line.

Measure down 1" on the center front. Connect this 1" down measurement to

the strap. Measure from the shoulder point down 5". Connect the strap to

the armhole with a curved line.

Darts. The underarm dart is made 5" down from the underarm, 1-1/2" wide,

and 3-1/2" long. To draw the waistline dart, follow the directions for simple

dress darts given earlier in the chapter.

Back . Draw a back torso. Draw the back bust line using the same formula,

bust measurement divided by 4 (36" divided by 4 = 9"). Measure from the

neck point over on the shoulder line 1-3/4", and make a strap 1" wide. Mea-

sure up 2" on the center back line from the back bust line. Draw a line across

the torso. Connect the strap to this line.

Skirt. To draw the skirt, start with the formula, waist measurement x 3 for

the skirt top. This is usually 2-1/2 or 3 yards long. Fold the material in

half lengthwise. Draw the length (24") add 3" for hem and 1" down the side

seam for the zipper. Make a mark 9" down from the skirt top for the zipper

position. Gather the top of the skirt to equal the waist measurement. Sew

skirt to bodice at the waistline.

Strap. Measure the front strap length and the back strap length to determine

how long to cut the strap. Cut the strap 1" wide.

Belt

Draw the belt making the length the waist measurement divided by 2 (28"

divided by 2 = 14") plus 6" for buckle and eyes.   Make the belt the same

width as the buckle used.   Add any style bodice.

Jumper Style Dress

Draw front torso. Extend the center front line to 40" for the dress length. At the center front make a mark 8" down from the neck point. Draw a line across the torso for the hip measurement which is determined by the formula, <u>hip measurement divided by 4.</u> Draw the waistline across using the measurement determined by the formula, <u>waist measurement divided by 4 plus 1".</u> Connect waistline to underarm with a curved ruler (curve inward). At the end of the length line draw a line across using the formula, <u>hip measurement divided by 4 plus 1/2",</u> for the A-line.

Using the curved ruler (curve outward) connect waistline point to hip line. Connect hip line to skirt length line with a straight ruler. From the neck point measure over on the shoulder line 1", measure down 8" on the center front, and connect these two marks with a straight line to complete the V neck. To draw the darts in this dress follow the same formulas used in making darts for the shift dress described earlier in this chapter. To draw the back of this dress, lay the front torso on the fabric and draw around the torso following the front torso except for the neck. Follow the neck from the original back torso.

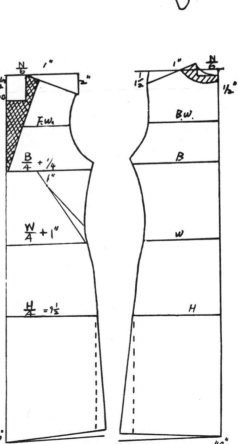

This style dress is buttoned down the center front.
Follow the directions for the simple shift dress with
two darts. Add 4" down the center front (3" for the
fold under and 1" for buttons). When drawing the
torso on the material, place the center front of the
torso on the selvedge edge of the material.

Collar. Draw a front torso. The collar for this
style is 2" wide. Following the formula for the
collar length, neck measurement divided by 2,
study the equation below:

14-1/2" divided by 2 = 7-1/4"

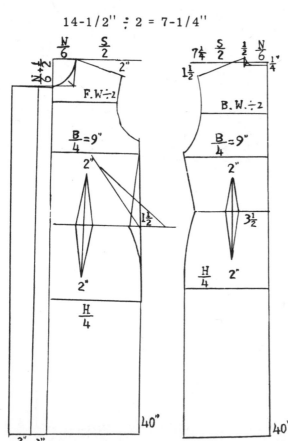

14-1/2" ÷ 2 = 7-1/4"

Draw the collar length line 7-1/4" long.
Draw a line on the right end of this line
2" up. On the left end of the length line
draw a line up 1/2", connect the 1/2"
point to collar length. Extend the top
left end of the collar 3/4". Connect
this 3/4" point to the 1/2" up point.
Connect the 3/4" point to the 2" width
on the right side of the collar.

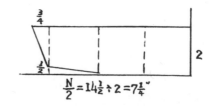

$\frac{N}{2} = 14\frac{1}{2} \div 2 = 7\frac{1}{4}$

Lay the cutout dress on the lining fabric and draw around the dress. Do not include the 3" hem allowance in the lining drawing. For the dress with a center front or center back opening, allow only 1" down the opening instead of 3".

Sew the entire dress together sewing in darts, sleeves and zipper. Do not sew facings (neck or sleeves) or hem the dress.

Sew the lining together sewing in darts, sleeves and hem.

Place wrong side of dress to wrong side of lining. Baste the lining to the dress around the neck (and armhole if the dress is sleeveless).

Sew the lining, dress and neck facings around the neck.

Turn the facing over the lining and hand sew to the lining. If the dress is sleeveless, sew the armhole of the dress, the lining, and the facing together. Turn the facing and hem to the lining around the armhole.

Turn the hem of the dress over the lining and hand sew to the lining.

To make the zipper opening in the lining, (down the center back or underarm) turn under the seam allowance on the lining of the zipper placket and hand sew around the edges.

Turn under seam allowance on the lining sleeve bottom and hand sew to the bottom of the dress sleeve.

11

Maternity Dresses

Maternity V Neck Jumper

This style jumper can be worn with or without a blouse. There is no waistline or hip line in this torso. Draw the front torso, extend the length 40" or desired length. To determine the position of the bust line follow the formula, <u>bust measurement divided by 4 + 1</u>. Using the measurements from the chart, 28" divided by 4 +1" = 8". Draw the bust line 10" down from the neck point and 8" across the torso. Extend the skirt bottom 2-1/2" at the hem line, measure up 1" on the hip side and connect this 1" point to the armhole with a straight line.

To draw the neckline measure over on the shoulder 1" from the neck point. Measure down the center front from the neck 4". Connect these two measurements with a straight line forming a V.

When drawing the armhole for a jumper style dress, use the measurement between the sleeveless and with sleeves measurement. For example, sleeveless = 16", with sleeves=18-1/2", for the jumper make the armhole 18".

Back

Draw a back torso.

Follow the formula:

<u>bust measurement</u>

divided by 4 +1". Make the bust line in the back torso the same as in the front.

Extend the skirt bottom the same as the front and make the armhole

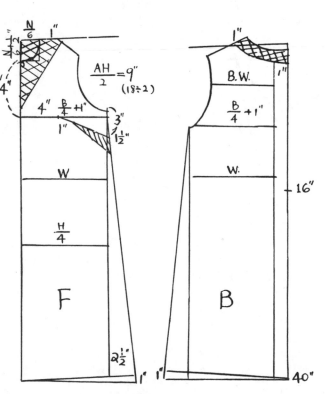

changes.

To draw the neck measure down 1" on center front line from the neck.   Measure over on the shoulder from the neck point 1".

Connect these two measurements with a curved line.

Add 1" seam allowance down the entire center back for the zipper.

Make a mark down 16" on the center back for the position of the zipper.

Simple Maternity Dress

This style dress has no opening but is pulled over the head. Draw a front torso using the measurements and formulas previously learned. To draw the front neck, measure over on the shoulder line from the neck point 2". Measure down the center front from the neck 2". Connect these two lines with a curved line. Draw an underarm dart down 4" from the underarm and make the dart 1-1/2" wide. The bottom of the dress should be extended 2-1/2". Measure up on the hip side 1/2", connect to the underarm with a straight line. Fold under the 2-1/2" extension, and iron to form a pleat. Three frog buttons are used on the side of the dress. The first frog is sewn 3" down from the underarm, and the second frog is sewn at the hip, and the other frog is sewn between the under-arm and hip. As the figure increases in size the frogs may be left unbuttoned as trimming. Frogs may be purchased in a trimming store.

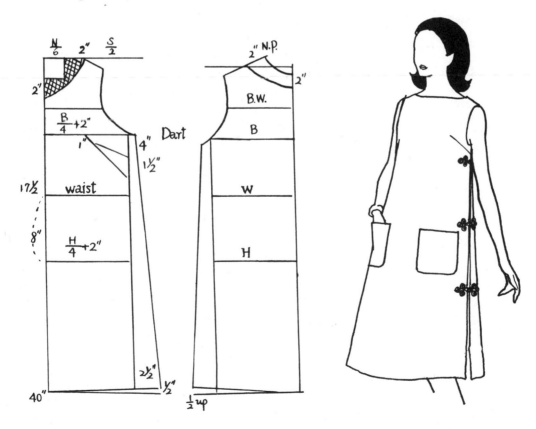

Draw a front torso.   Measure hip, make the blouse as wide as the hip measurement plus 2" to allow for increased size as the baby grows.   Draw a straight line from the neck point down 24" for the entire length of the blouse.   This length is the same for all sizes.

To draw the darts in this style blouse, measure from the neck point to the bust point and draw a line across 4" to the center front.   From the armhole measure down 4", make a mark and connect to the bust point.   Make another mark down 1-1/2" on the underarm side, and connect this mark to the bust point with a straight line forming the dart.

Skirt

Copy the straight skirt front previously learned.   To draw the skirt back copy the back straight skirt, but on the hip edge add 4" the entire length of the skirt.   Measure down 10" from the waist, and trim out 4" down to the length of the skirt because the extra 4" is only needed in the hip area.   No zipper is sewn in this skirt, but instead both sides are left open 8" down from the waist.

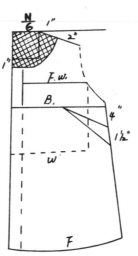

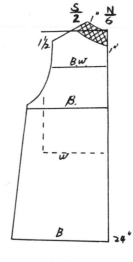

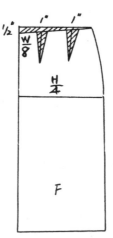

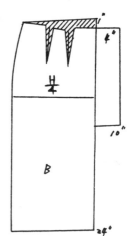

Band for the Maternity Skirt

Measure around the front and back skirt waist and add 1" for the length of the skirt band.   Make the band 3" wide.

On the skirt front band, sew two buttonholes on each end of the band, and sew to the top of the skirt front.   On the back skirt sew the entire band to the top of the skirt.   Fold the back skirt in 4" on each side, and sew three buttons on each end of the skirt band 1" apart.   As size increases, move the skirt to the next button.

After the baby is born, this skirt can be altered to a straight skirt by following the directions for drawing a straight skirt in this book.   No hole has been cut in this skirt front style, which makes this alteration possible.

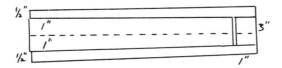

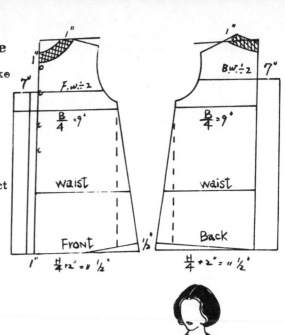

Gathered Maternity Blouse

Pleated or Gathered Maternity Blouse

This style will be made in two pieces, the yoke section and the pleated section. Draw a front torso. Measure down from the neck 1" on the center front. Measure over on the shoulder line 1" from the neck point. Connect these two measurements with a curved line. Draw a straight line from the armhole down 24" for the length, and make the width of the blouse the hip measurement plus 2".

Copy the front width line from the original front torso. Place this torso on the material with the center front on the fold of the material, add 1" for seams above the cut line and cut around the torso. To draw the pleated section of the torso, extend the front width line 7" at the center front for pleats. The 7" extension is placed on the fold of the material. This extension can be gathered or pleated as desired. To figure the pleats, subtract the front width measurement from the width of the material. As shown in the drawing 14" plus the front width measurement (which is 14") equals 28". 28" minus 14" = 14".

Each pleat is 1", so according to the above figures there will be 7 pleats in the front

torso and 7 pleats in the back·torso.

Fold the torso with a 1" pleat on top and a 1" pleat inside, and have this torso fit the yoke torso just drawn.

Back

Draw the back torso the same as the front except add 3" down the center back for the fold-under and buttons, since this style is buttoned down the back.

This same style may be used for a maternity dress by extending the length.

Take accurate measurements and follow any of the blouse styles described in Chapter 8.

Draw all the blouses 24" long from the neck point. On both the front and back torsos draw the bottom width of the blouse the hip measurement plus 2". Study the illustrations below which show three different collars.

To draw a torso for maternity slacks and shorts, follow the directions given in Chapter 9. The only changes are made in the back torso. Extend the zipper side of the back pattern 4". Follow the directions given for the maternity skirt and waist band. Make shorts the desired length.

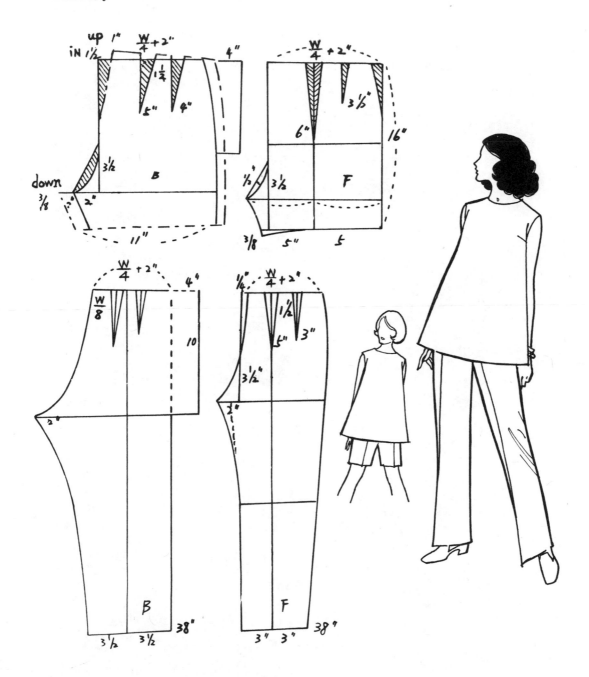

12

Evening Dresses

Off Shoulder Style Evening Dress

A paper pattern should be made for this style dress
and placed on the fabric before cutting to avoid cutting the fabric incorrectly.   Measure the length from
the neck point to the ankle, draw a front torso and
extend the center front line the length of this measurement.   The medium is usually 54" long.   Draw the
waistline across the torso using the formula, waistline divided by 4 + 1" for dart.   Connect the armhole
to the waistline with a curved ruler (curve inward).
Draw the hip 8" down and 9-1/2" (for average hip
measure) across (38" divided by 4 = 9-1/2"). Connect
waistline to hip line with a curved ruler (curve outward).   The formula to determine the amount to taper
an evening skirt bottom is:

hip measurement divided by 4 minus 1-1/2"

In this drawing 38" divided by 4 minus 1-1/2" = 8". To draw the darts, follow
the same directions for marking darts in the shift dress in Chapter 10. Measure across the skirt length line 8", connect with a straight line to the hip
line. This torso is drawn so the center front is on the fold. Open the pattern,
draw a straight line on the blouse front paper pattern from neck point to the
armhole. Either left or right shoulder may be cut away.

Lay this paper pattern on the fabric, add 1/2" seam along the cut line from
neck point to armhole.

Back

To make the back pattern draw a back torso and follow the same directions used for the front torso except to extend the center back line, taper the skirt, draw in the waistline, hip line, darts, and cut the shoulder away. A 12" side zipper is used in this style dress. Sew a hook and eye at the zipper top. Measure from the skirt length up 16", and leave open for the slit. The formula to follow for the slit opening is:

16" up from the skirt bottom

This slit may be in the center back or front or side of the skirt. If the bottom of the skirt is drawn straight down and not tapered, no slit is made. Whenever the skirt is tapered, the skirt must be slit. If the slit is made down the center front or back, add 1" down the front or back for the fold-under. Sew the skirt down to the 16" slit.

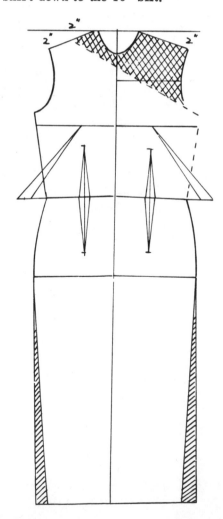

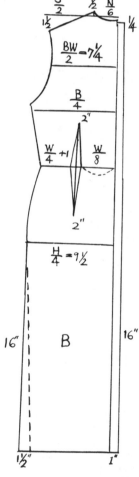

This style dress may be slit down the side or center back as desired. Add 1"
down the center back from the neck for the 22" zipper. Follow the illustrations.
Draw a front torso using directions for the shift dress explained in Chapter 10.
No changes are made in the neck, so follow the same neck as in the front and
back torso. Extend the center front to 54" or desired length. Taper skirt
bottom at the hip side 1-1/2". Measure up 1/2" and connect to the hip line
with a straight line.

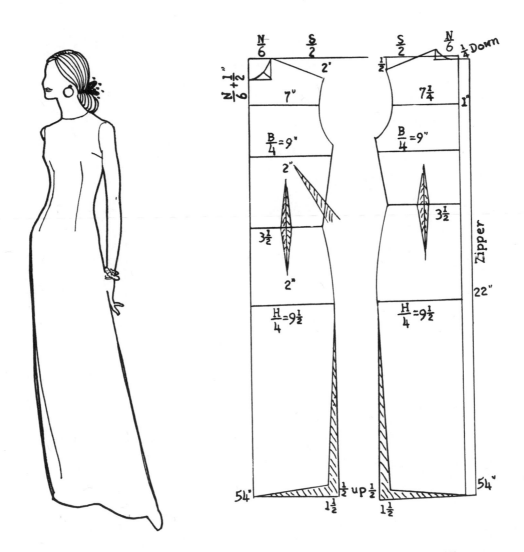

Evening Dress with a Cut Waist $\frac{N}{6}+\frac{1}{2}$"

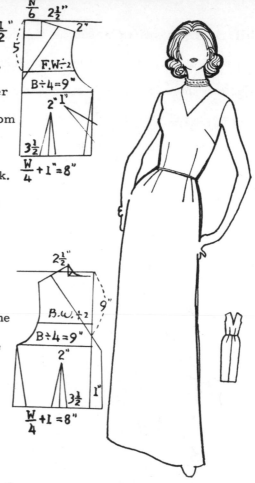

Draw a front torso. For the low neck style, measure down 5" from the neck on the center front, measure over on the shoulder line from the neck point 2-1/2". Connect these two points with a straight line to form the V neck. To draw the darts follow the same formulas and drawings learned in Chapter 10 for the cut waistline style.

Back

Draw a back torso with the center back on the selvedge of the material. And add 1" on the center back because this style has a zipper in the back. Measure down the center back from the neck 9". Measure from the neck point across the shoulder 2-1/2". Connect these two points with a straight line to form the V at the neck. Draw in back waistline darts and armhole.

To draw the skirt, follow the front straight skirt explained in Chapter 7. Extend the center front for the length line, and taper the skirt 1-1/2" as shown in the drawing. Instead of making darts in the skirt gather the fabric from the beginning of the first dart to the end of the second dart using the dart

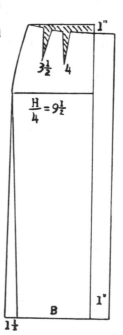

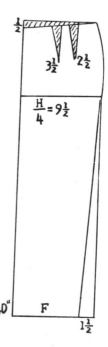

positions learned in the cut waist style dress. The skirt back is made the same

as the front. Add piping along waistline when sewing bodice to skirt.

A-Line Style Evening Dress

To draw the bodice of this dress draw a front torso.

Measure over on the shoulder line from neck point

3-1/2". Measure from the neck down the center

front 3". Connect these two measurements with a

curved line. Follow previous directions and draw

the waistline dart, bust line dart and mark waistline

measurement, as well as the sleeveless armhole.

Back

Draw a back torso. Measure down 6" on the center

back from the neck, and measure over on the shoulder

line from neck point 3-1/2". Connect these points

with a curved line. Draw in waistline dart, and waist-

line measurement and armhole.

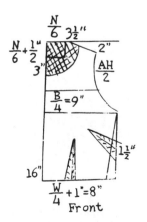

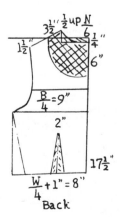

<u>Skirt</u> (for A-Line style evening dress)

An A-line style skirt can be used

for evening dresses. To draw the

A-line, extend the skirt bottom 3",

up 1" and connect to the hip with a

straight line. Follow directions

used for the straight skirt and draw

darts.

Before sewing bodice to the skirt

insert piping along the waistline.

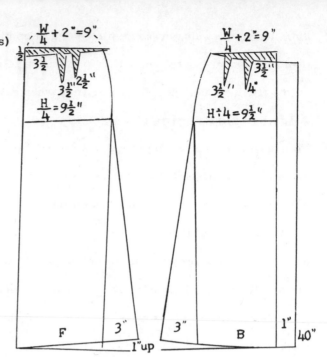

Any straight skirt may be used for an evening dress by extending the entire length 40" or to the ankle, and tapering the skirt bottom 1-1/2". This skirt is slit at the center back.

Follow the blouse illustrated or any blouse may be worn with the skirt. For other blouse ideas turn to Chapter 8.

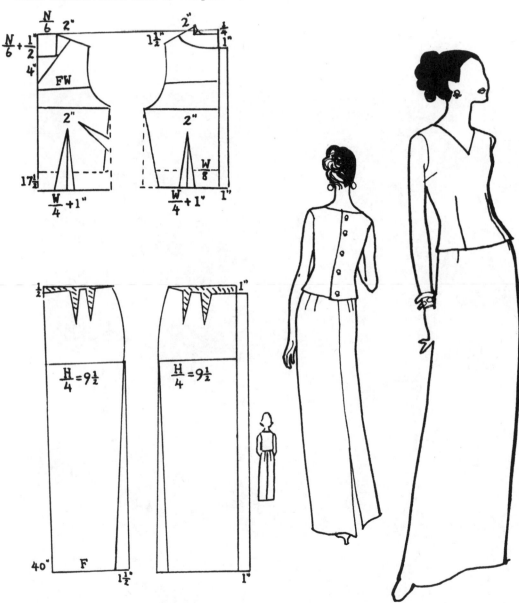

13

Suits

Basic Suits

Suits are made 2" larger through the bust than the regular torso. Jackets may be drawn longer by extending front and underarm lines. Follow this formula for the extra width: bust measurement divided by 4 + 1/2".

Add length to the torso because the jacket is longer. This length is made from 4" to 6" down from the waist as desired. Adjust the armhole of the front torso as mentioned previously to allow for sleeves (armhole measurement plus 2-1/2" divided by 2 = size to make front armhole).

Using the chart measurements, 16" + 2-1/2" divided by 2 = 9-1/4". Draw the jack front following the formula above for the bust line width and armhole. Draw in the darts.

Back

The back jacket is made like the front, adjusting the armhole and length and following the bust line formula.

Sleeves

The short, 3/4 or long

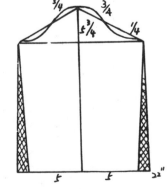

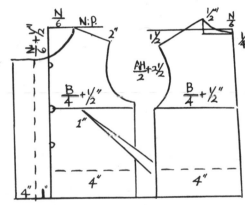

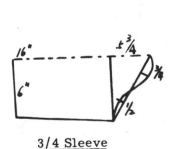

3/4 Sleeve

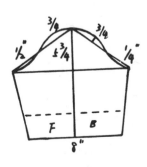

Short Sleeve

Long Sleeve

sleeve may be used with this suit. The long sleeve is made 5" wide at the bottom instead of 6" as in the 3/4 sleeve because the sleeve is small at the wrist.

Collar for the Basic Suit

Draw a length line according to the formula, <u>F. N. +B. N. divided by 2</u> (14-1/2" divided by 2 = 7-1/4"). On the right side, draw a line up 3". Connect the 3" line to the length line. At the top left edge of the collar, extend the line 1/2". Connect this 1/2" up point from the collar length line. Divide the collar length line into thirds. Connect the 1/2" up point at the left corner to the first division as shown in the diagram.

Skirt

Draw a straight skirt.

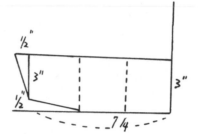

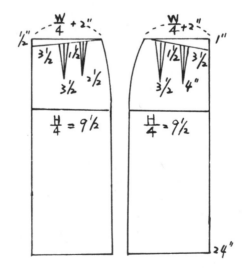

Draw a front torso. Draw bust line following the formula, extend the center front line to measure 22" from the neck, and make the side from underarm longer to connect across to the center front extension. Add 3" on both fronts at center front for the fold-under and buttons. To cut the neck facings for this suit, refer to the description given for drawing neck facings in Chapter 8. To draw the neck, measure down 5" from the neck on the center front. Measure over on the shoulder 1" from neck point. Connect these two measurements to form a V neck.

Darts

Measure down 5" from the underarm, and make a dart 1-1/2" wide. Dart point is 1" down from the bust point. The shoulder dart is 2", make a 1/2" dart (1/4" each side of center of the dart). Make the dart point 1-1/2" up from the bust tip.

Pocket

For the flap or false pocket, cut a strip of material 5" wide and 5" long. Fold in half. Sew pocket 1" up from open edge to the jacket. Fold pocket over stitching making outside measurement 1-1/2" and inside measurement 1".

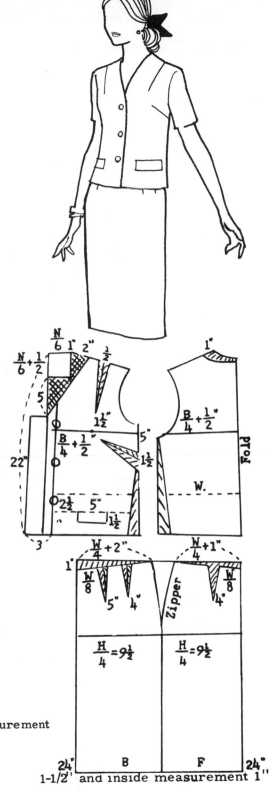

<u>Lining</u>

To line the jacket follow the directions on page 160 for lining a coat.

<u>Back</u>

Draw a back torso. Draw the neck by measuring over from neck point

on the shoulder line 1" and connecting to the center back neck.

Finish the back the same as the front.

<u>Sleeves</u>

Follow directions for short sleeves on page 45.

<u>Skirt</u>

Follow the straight skirt directions on page 69.

Classic Suit

Draw a front torso, add 3" to the bottom to make the jacket longer, follow the formula: <u>bust measurement divided by 4 + 1/2"</u>. To draw the neck line, measure down 1" on center front from the neck point and measure over 1/2" from neck point across the shoulder line. Connect these two points with a curved line. Add 3" down the center front for buttons.

Dart

To draw the underarm dart, measure down 5" from the armhole and make a mark, measure over 4" on the bust line and down 1". Connect this dart point to the 5" mark with a straight line. Draw another straight line from the bust point to a point 1-1/2" down from the 5" mark on the underarm side.

Back

Draw a back torso, add 3" to the bottom of the jacket, and follow the formula used for the front. Add the waistline dart.

To draw the neck, measure over from neck point on the shoulder line 1/2", and connect to the back neck with a curved line.

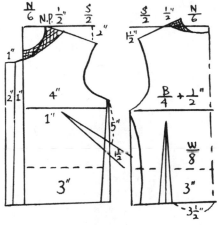

Sleeve

Draw a 3/4 sleeve.

Collar

Follow the collar directions on page 61, blouse with a square collar.

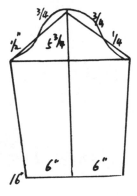

Skirt

Follow the directions for the front straight skirt, except make only one dart using the formula, <u>waist measurement divided by 4 + 1</u>, to determine the waist measurement.

Back

The skirt back is made the same as the front except the dart is 1" wide and 5" long.

Follow directions for lining a suit on page 160.

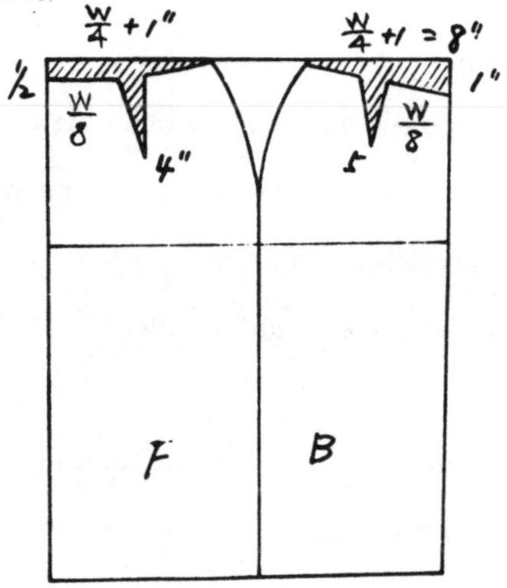

Draw a front torso, make armhole adjustments for sleeves.
Draw bust line following formula, extend the jacket length
3". To draw the neck, measure up 1" from the bust line,
and measure over from neck point on the shoulder line 1".
Connect these two points to form a V neck.

To draw the curve on the front jacket bottom, extend
the front torso 3" as already directed. At the corner
on the center front make a line in 1", measure up
on the center front line 1-1/2" and measure across
the front torso 2" from the center front. Connect
the 1-1/2" point on the center front through the 1"
line, to the 2" point with a curved line. Trim out
the point originally drawn in the torso.

Draw in underarm dart.

<u>Back</u>

Draw a back torso. Extend the jacket length

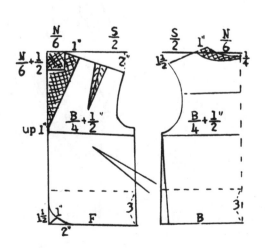

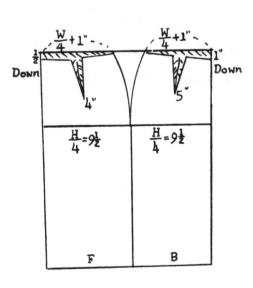

3" and finish the same as the front. To draw the neck, measure over 1" on the shoulder line from the neck point and connect to the center back neck.

Bow

Cut a strip of material 3-1/2" wide and 5" long.

Skirt

Draw a straight skirt with one dart. Line the suit according to directions on page 160.

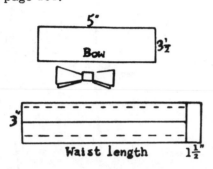

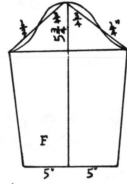

Chinese Mandarin Collar Suit

This style suit is open down the front with four pairs of Chinese Frogs as trimming. Frogs may be purchased at a trimming shop. Follow the directions for lining on page 157. Draw a front torso, do not change neck. Follow the formula, bust measurement divided by 4 + 1/2", used for making the suit large enough to line and wear over a blouse. Add 3" down the center front for buttons. The length of the jacket is 4" longer than the torso, so add the 4" to the bottom of the torso.

Darts

Follow the illustration to make the darts.

Back

Draw a back torso following the formula, bust measurement divided by 4 + 1/2".

Do not change the neck, and add the 4" to the length of the jacket.

Collar

Follow the directions for making the collar from the blouse with the mandarin collar on page 99.

Sleeves

Draw a 3/4 or long sleeve.

Skirt

Follow the directions for the straight skirt with one dart.

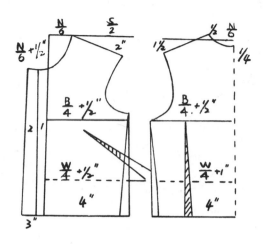

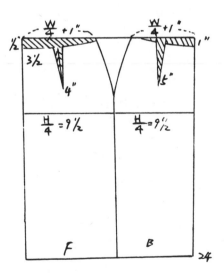

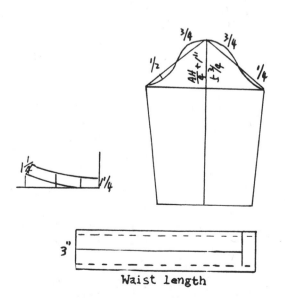

Waist length

Vest

Vests may be fitted and the bottom designed in a pointed or curved style.
Draw a front torso, adjust torso to desired length. Follow formula,
bust measurement divided by 4 + 1/2", add 2" down center for facing.
The armhole must be made larger because this style jacket
will be worn over a blouse or sweater. Follow the formula,
armhole measurement + 2-1/2" divided by 2 (16" + 2-1/2"
divided by 2 = 9-1/4"). To draw neck, measure down center
front from the neck 5". Measure over on shoulder line 1/2".
Connect these two points with a straight line. Make facings
for neck and sleeves.

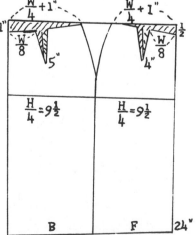

Darts

Follow directions for making darts as explained
on page 146.

Back

Draw a back torso, adjust armhole, draw in
bust line according to the formula followed
for the front.

To draw the neck, follow the drawing and measure over on shoulder line 1/2" from the
neck point. Connect to the back neck with a
curved line.

Skirt

Follow the straight or A-line skirt, whichever
desired. Line the suit according to the directions
on page 160.

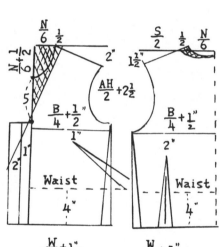

14

Coats

Coats

The entire coat has 9" more through the bust than the regular torso so that it may be worn over suits and dresses.

The following formulas must be followed when drawing a coat:

1) for the length of the front bust line in all coats regardless of size:

bust measurement divided by 4 + 2-1/2"

2) for the length of the back bust line in all coats regardless of size:

bust measurement divided by 4 + 2"

3) for the front width: (when drawing coat, it is not necessary to measure front width)
bust measurement divided by 6 + 3/4"

4) for the size of armhole in all coats regardless of size:

armhole measurement + 4 divided by 2

To determine the amount to add down the center front, measure the button to be used. If the button is 1" allow 2" for buttons and 4" for fold-under. The coat length is always 1" longer than the dress.

Coat Front—Chesterfield Style

Draw a front torso. Follow formula, B. divided by 4 + 2-1/2" (36 divided by 4 = 9 + 2-1/2" = 11-1/2"). Draw the bust line 11-1/2" long and 10" down from neck point. No changes are made in the neck from original torso. Draw the front width line following the formula, B. divided by 6 + 3/4" (36" divided by 6 + 3/4"= 6-3/4"). Draw the front width 6-3/4" long and down 3" from neck point. Add 6" down center front for buttons and fold under. Add 1" to length (make length 41" following chart measurements.)

Armhole

Follow the formula, A. H. + 4 divided by 2 (16 + 4 divided by 2 = 10")

Adjust the armhole on the torso to 10". Measure down 3/4" from bust line.

Connect this point to the armhole. Connect the underarm to the hem with a

straight line.

Dart

Measure over on the shoulder line from neck point 2". Make a dart 1" wide

and from the bust line up 2" for the dart point. Connect with straight lines to

form the dart.

Draw the waistline on the torso following the front waist length (17-1/2").

Measure from neck point down 17-1/2". The length of the waistline is the same

as the bust line.

Pocket

Measure 4" from the center front on the waistline for position of the pocket.

Make the pocket 6" long and 2-1/2" wide. Round the corners of the pocket.

Another method to follow to determine pocket position is, measure 9" down

from bust line.

Extend the skirt bottom 2" or 3" and up 1/2". Connect to the underarm point

with a straight line.

Measure down from bust line 2-1/2" and place the first button. The

remaining two buttons are placed 5" apart down the center front.

Back

Draw a back torso. Do not change the neck. Draw the back width the same as

the front width. Draw the same armhole as the front. To determine the length

of the back bust line follow the formula, B. divided by 4 + 2, instead of +2-1/2"

as in front bust line (36" divided by 4+2"=11"). Draw back bust line 11" long and 10" down from neck point.

Change the length to 41".

Dart

Measure over from neck point 2" on shoulder line for the shoulder dart.

Make the dart 1/2" wide and 2" up from the back width line.

Extend the bottom of the coat 1-1/2" or 2-1/2" up 1/2". Connect to the armhole with a straight line.

Sleeves

Study the picture and draw a long sleeve. Change the sleeve cap length from 5-3/4" to 6" because of the larger armhole. Draw the line from A to D 6" long. Draw the line A to C 10" long. Draw in sleeve curve the same as previously learned.

The sleeve length is 22", but add 2" to the sleeve bottom for the hem.

Collar

Follow the directions and illustrations for the shirt collar. When coat is finished, the collar is folded 3/4" from neck point over on the shoulder line.

Pocket

Draw the pocket 7" long and 7" wide. Sew pocket on all edges, turn. Fold pocket in half. Measure up from the bottom 1" and sew pocket to the coat across this 1" line. Fold top of pocket over this line.

Lining for Coat

To draw the coat lining, draw the coat front and back except do not add the extension down the center front for buttons and fold-under. Do not add the hem allowance (3") in the lining.

Sew the entire coat together, sewing in the sleeves and hem. Do not sew facings.

Sew the entire lining together, sewing in the sleeves and hem.

Place the wrong side of the coat to the wrong side of the lining and baste around the neck.

Baste lining to the coat along side seams with long loose stitches.

Sew lining, coat, and facings together. Turn facing and hand sew to the lining.

Turn under lining sleeve allowance at the sleeve bottom and hand sew to the coat sleeve.

Hostess Coat

A hostess coat can be drawn from the diagrams shown earlier in this chapter.

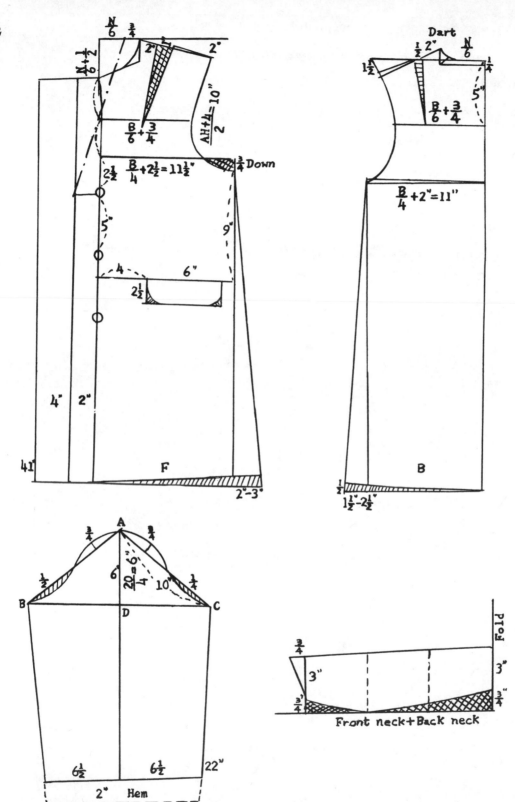

$$\frac{N}{6} \quad \frac{3}{4}$$

$$\frac{N}{6}+\frac{1}{2}$$

2"

2"

$$\frac{B}{6}+\frac{3}{4}$$

$$\frac{AH+4}{2}=10"$$

$$\frac{3}{4}\text{ Down}$$

$$2\frac{1}{2} \quad \frac{B}{4}+2\frac{1}{2}=11\frac{1}{2}"$$

5"

9"

4

6"

$$2\frac{1}{2}$$

4" 2"

41" F

2"-3"

Dart

$$\frac{1}{2} \; 2" \quad \frac{N}{6}$$

$$1\frac{1}{2} \qquad \frac{1}{4}$$

$$\frac{B}{6}+\frac{3}{4}$$

5"

$$\frac{B}{4}+2"=11"$$

B

$$\frac{1}{2}$$

$$1\frac{1}{2}"-2\frac{1}{2}"$$

A

$$\frac{3}{4} \qquad \frac{3}{4}$$

$$\frac{1}{2} \qquad 6" \qquad \frac{3}{4}$$

$$\frac{20}{4}=6" \qquad 10"$$

B D C

$$6\frac{1}{2} \qquad 6\frac{1}{2} \qquad 22"$$

2" Hem

$$\frac{3}{4}$$

3" Fold

$$\frac{3}{4} \qquad 3"$$

$$\frac{3}{4}$$

Front neck+Back neck

Draw a front torso. To draw the neck, measure down the center front from the neck 1". Measure across from neck point on the shoulder 1". Connect with a curved line.

Draw the front width line following the formula, <u>bust measurement divided by 6 + 3/4"</u> (36 divided by 6 + 3/4" = 6-3/4").

Draw the bust line usi ng the formula, <u>bust measurement divided by 4 + 2-1/2"</u> (36" divided by 4 + 3-1/2" = ll-1/2").

Dart

Make the shoulder dart 1" over from the new neck, and make the dart 1" wide and as long as the front width line. Draw the armhole 1" down, connect to the armhole. Add 4" down the entire center front. Extend the skirt bottom 2" up 1/2". Connect to the armhole.

Back

Draw the back torso. To draw the neck, measure over on the shoulder line 1" from neck point. Connect to the center back neck.

No change is made in the armhole from the original torso.

Draw in back width and bust line the same as done fo r the front.

Dart

Measure over 1" from the new neck, make a dart 1" wide and 4" long. When drawing the dart. Place the ruler so it touches the back bust line point (which is 4" over from the center back) and draw a straight line 4" down from the shoulder dart measurement.)

<u>Sleeve.</u> Draw a long sleeve.

<u>Collar</u>

Use paper to draw this collar.

Draw the front new neck including the armhole on paper.

Measure from neck point over on the shoulder line 1-1/4". Measure down on center front 1-1/4". Connect with a curved line.

Extend both lines 1-1/2" at the center front making the entire collar 1-1/4" wide. Draw a back new neck on paper. Measure down 1-1/4" from the neck at the center back, and measure across from neck point on shoulder line 1-1/4". Connect these two points with a curved line.

Lay paper on the fabric and cut out the collar.

Sew one button on the coat just below the collar and a snap on the collar.

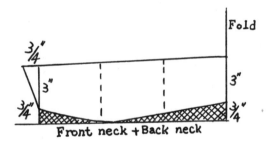

Front neck + Back neck

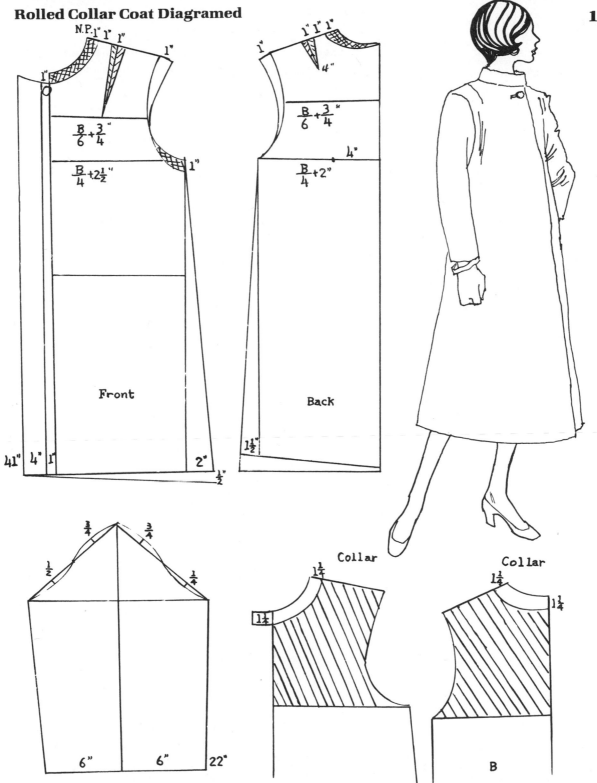

N.P. 1" 1" 1"

1"

1"

$\frac{B}{6}+\frac{3}{4}$"

$\frac{B}{4}+2\frac{1}{2}$"

1"

Front

41" 4" 1"

2"

$\frac{1}{2}$"

1" 1" 1"

1"

4"

$\frac{B}{6}+\frac{3}{4}$"

$\frac{B}{4}+2$"

4"

Back

$1\frac{1}{2}$"

$\frac{3}{4}$ $\frac{3}{4}$

$\frac{1}{2}$ $\frac{1}{4}$

6"   6"   22"

Collar

$1\frac{1}{4}$

$1\frac{1}{4}$

Collar

$1\frac{1}{4}$

$1\frac{1}{4}$

B

Simple Coat

Draw a front torso. To draw the neck, measure from the neck down the center front 1". Measure from neck point across the shoulder line 1/2". Connect these two points with a curved line.

Make the front dart, draw the front width, bust line, armhole waistline, pocket and bottom extension the same as for the Chesterfield Coat.

Back

Draw a back torso. To draw the neck, measure from neck point across the shoulder line 1/2". Connect to the center back neck with a curved line.

Draw front width, bust line, armhole and bottom extension the same as the coat front.

Sleeves

Make the same sleeves as for the Chesterfield Coat.

Buttons

The first button is placed 1" down the center front from the neck. The four remaining buttons are placed 5" apart down the center front.

Collar

Study the drawing and draw the collar. To make the corner of the collar round, measure in 1" at the top left corner and trim out the point.

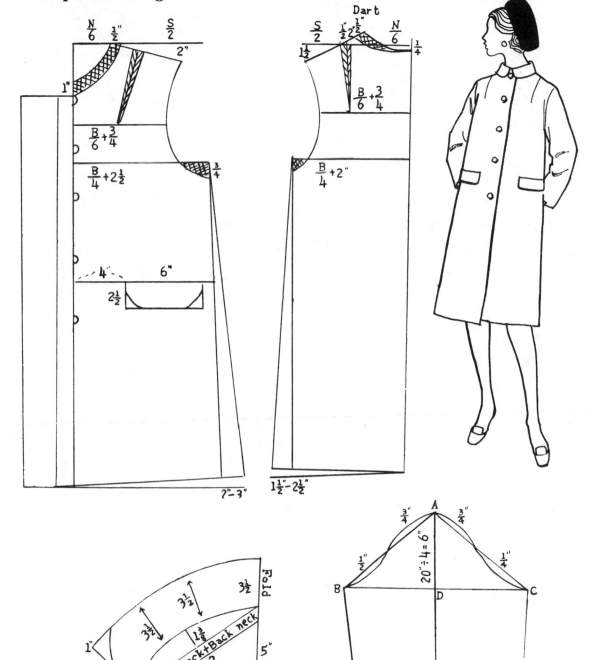

This style coat is made cocktail or evening dress length with no buttons, no collar, and 3/4 length sleeves. To draw the coat, draw a front torso. To draw the neck, measure down the center front from the neck 1". Measure across from neck point across shoulder 1". Connect these two points with a curved line.

Armhole

Measure down 1" from the regular armhole and connect this point to the regular armhole. Follow the formula for bust line width, B. divided by 4 + 2-1/2", and draw the bust line. Do not add down the center front. Draw the waistline by measuring down the center front from the neck the distance equal to the front waistline length measurement (17-1/2" average).

Dart. On the armhole edge make a measurement on the bust line 3/4" wide for the dart and 7" from center front on the waistline. Continue the dart to the hip line (8" below the waistline). Draw another line 3/4" over at the armhole to the hip line. At the waistline make this line 1/2" wide and form a dart point at the hip line.

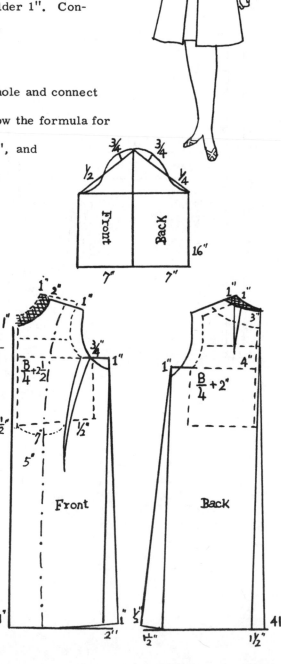

The dart shown in the diagram can be used in any of the styles to make the coat fitted or a dart can be drawn in any of these styles.

Facing

Measure over on the shoulder line from the new neck point 2". Measure over from the center front 5" all along the front. Connect these 5" measurements to the 2" shoulder to form the facing. Copy this facing on paper and lay paper on the fabric and cut out.

Extend the coat bottom 2" up 1". Connect to the 1" down point at the armhole with a straight line making the coat 1" longer in length.

Back

Draw a back torso. To draw the neck, measure over on the shoulder 1" from neck point. Connect to the center back neck with a curved line.

Draw bust line width the same as the front. Draw the armhole 1" down at the armhole edge as done for the front.

Dart

Measure from the neck center back 3" over on the shoulder line and make a 1" dart. Draw the dart length to the back width line.

Skirt

Extend the skirt bottom 1-1/2" up 1/2". Connect with a straight line to the armhole. Make the 1" additional length the same as the front.

The flare in the coat is made by extending the center back 1-1/2" at the bottom and connecting to the center back neck.

Sleeves

Follow directions for a 3/4 sleeve.

Follow the directions for the cocktail coat except extend the center front line

the desired length.   54" is the length used in the drawing for the medium size.

Measure up 1/2" at the bottom of the coat, connect to the underarm.   Add

2" hem and seam allowances before cutting.

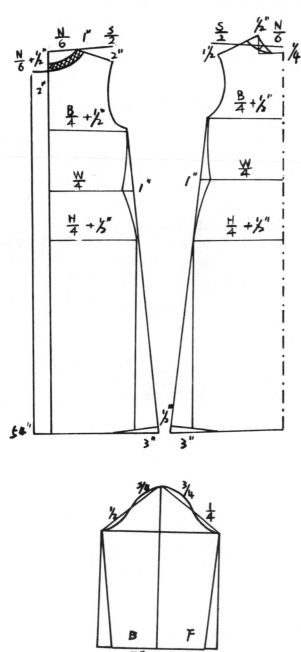

15

Everyday Fashions

Bathrobe

Draw a front torso. Make the length (41") or desired length. No change is made in the neck of the original torso. Draw the front width line using the formula, B. divided by 6 + 3/4" (36" divided by 6 + 3/4" = 6 -3 /4"). Draw the bust line using the formula, B. divided by 4 + 2-1/2"(36" divided by 4 + 2-1/2" = 11-1/2")

Dart

Make an underarm dart 2" down from the underarm and 1-1/2" wide. Measure over 5" from the center front for the dart point.

Collar

Measure the back neck on the original torso. Using the neck measurement from the chart (14-1/2"), the back neck is 6-1/4". Follow the drawing on page 174. Draw a slanted line 6-1/4" from the front neck. Draw a right angle line 4-1/2" across. Extend the skirt bottom 4" on the center front. Connect the 4-1/2" width at the neck to the skirt extension.

Pocket

Use the formula, waist measurement divided by 8 (28" divided by 8=3-1/2") and draw the waistline. Measure over 3-1/2" from the center front on the wasitline to determine position of the pocket. Make a square pocket 7" wide and 8-1/2" long. Sew the pocket on all edges, turn. Fold top of the pocket over 2-1/4", stitch 1/2" around the pocket. On hip side, measure up 1/2" at skirt bottom and connect to the armhole.

Facing

To make the facing, copy the entire collar on paper, lay the paper on the fabric and cut out.

Back

Draw a back torso. Make no changes in the neck from the original torso.

Measure down 1" at the armhole. Connect this point to the remaining armhole.

Draw the back width line using the formula, B. divided by 6 + 3/4"(36" divided

by 6 + 3/4"= 6-3/4"). Draw the back bust line using the formula, B. divided

by 4+ 2" (36" divided by 4 + 2"= 11"). Extend the length 41" or desired length.

Measure up 1/2" at the skirt bottom on the center front and connect to the arm-

hole with a straight line.

Sleeves

Draw a short, 3/4, or long sleeve as desired.

Belt

Use the formula, waist measurement x 2, to determine length of the belt.

Make the belt 2" wide. Extend the belt 1-1/2" at the top line and connect to

the bottom with a slanted line to form a point at the ends of the belt.

Bathrobe Diagramed

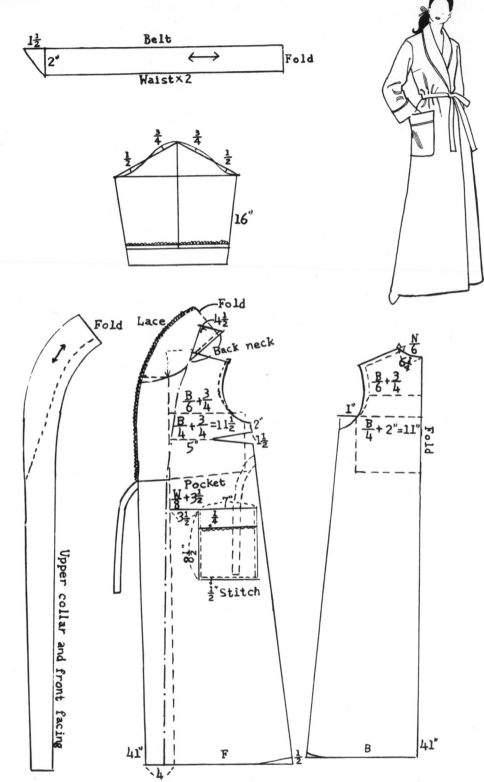

Belt

$1\frac{1}{2}$

2"

Fold

Waist × 2

$\frac{3}{4}$ $\frac{3}{4}$

$\frac{1}{2}$ $\frac{1}{2}$

16"

Fold

Lace

Fold

$4\frac{1}{2}$

Back neck

$\frac{B}{6}+\frac{3}{4}$

$\frac{B}{4}+\frac{3}{4}=11\frac{1}{2}$ 2"

5" $1\frac{1}{2}$

Pocket

$\frac{W}{8}+3\frac{1}{2}$ 7"

$3\frac{1}{2}$ $\frac{1}{4}$

$8\frac{1}{2}$

$\frac{1}{2}$"Stitch

Upper collar and front facing

41"   F $\frac{1}{2}$

4

$\frac{N}{6}$

$6\frac{1}{4}$

$\frac{B}{6}+\frac{3}{4}$

1"

$\frac{B}{4}+2"=11"$

Fold

B   41"

Play Suit

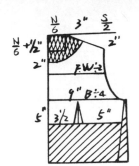
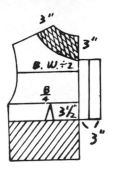

Draw a front torso. To draw the neck, measure down 2" from the neck on the center front. Measure from neck point across the shoulder 3". Connect these two points with a curved line. When making this suit for a child, do not make the bust dart. To make the bust dart for an adult use the formula, <u>waist measurement divided by 8</u> (28" divided by 8= 3-1/2"). Draw the dart 3-1/2" over from the center front. Draw in the front width line and bust line. Cut off the bottom at the line drawn 5" down from the bust line.

<u>Back</u>

Draw a back torso. Measure down the center back 3" from the neck and connect to a point 3" over from neck point on the shoulder line with a curved line. Add 3" down the center back for buttons and fold-under. Draw in the back width line, back bust line, and dart. Trim away the bottom of the torso to match the length of the front torso.

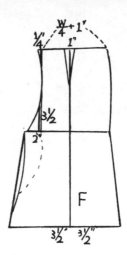

Pants

Follow the Bermuda Shorts directions
on page 109. A ruffle may be sewn on
the shorts bottom. The ruffle is made to
equal the measurement around the leg x 3.
Make the ruffle 3" wide, add 1/2" all around
the ruffle for seams.

Knickers

Follow the Bermuda Shorts directions on page 109. Extend the bottom
of the knickers and add length to the leg as shown in the diagram.
If less fullness is required, add less than 2". Measure the entire
amounts of both front and back with a tape measure. Try this amount
on your leg to determine the desired fullness. Extend the length
of the leg by 1". Make a casing, cut a piece of elastic equal to the
leg measurement and insert in casing.

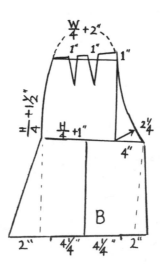

Bathing Suit

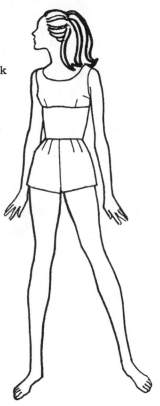

Draw a front torso. To draw the neck, measure from the neck point across the shoulder line 3". Measure from the neck down the center front 3". Connect these two points with a curved line. To draw the strap, measure from shoulder point in 1". Connect to armhole with a curved line. Draw in front width line, and underarm dart. Measure from the bust line down 5", trim away the bottom of the torso.

Dart

To draw the dart, draw a line across the torso 5" down from bust line and make a 1" dart over 4" from the center front. Measure from the bust line down 2" for the dart point and length of dart. Connect the dart point to the 5" line with straight lines to complete the underarm dart. Use the formula, <u>waistline divided by 4 + 1"</u>, to draw the waistline length. Connect this measurement to the armhole with a straight line.

Back

Draw a back torso. To draw the neck measure over from neck point on shoulder line 3". Measure down from the neck on the center back. Connect these two points with a curved line. Measure in 1" from the shoulder point. Connect to the armhole with a curved line. Add 3" down the center back

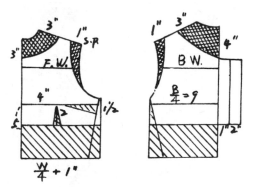

<u>Bathing Suit</u> (continued)

for buttons and fold-under. Cut off the bottom of the torso the same as the front which was 5" down from the bust line.

<u>Shorts</u>

Follow shorts directions on page 109.

<u>Bikini Suit</u>

To make a bikini, shorten the shorts length, add 1" for casing but do not alter the crotch drawing. Do not sew in the darts but leave the fullness. Make a casing, insert elastic.

To make the top, draw a curve from strap and dip at center front.

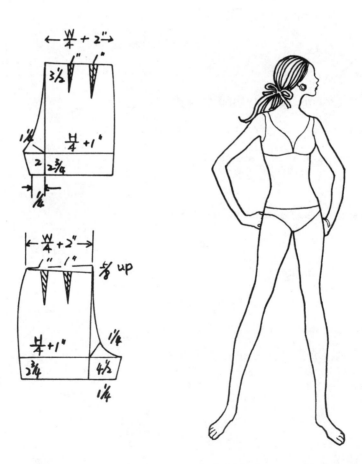

16

Children's Measurements

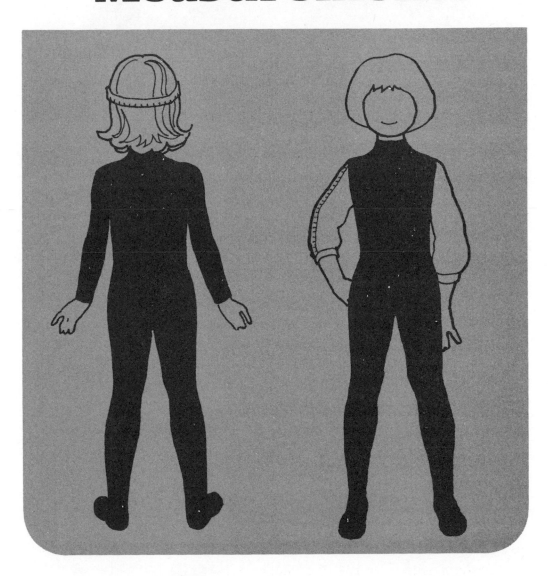

Taking Children's Measurements (Children ages 1 - 12)

Follow the directions and drawings for taking children's measurements.

These measurements will be used to draw the torsos.

1. <u>Neck</u>. Measure around the front neck

   joint lightly passing around the

   top of the back bone at the back

   and inner part of the collarbone

   at the front.

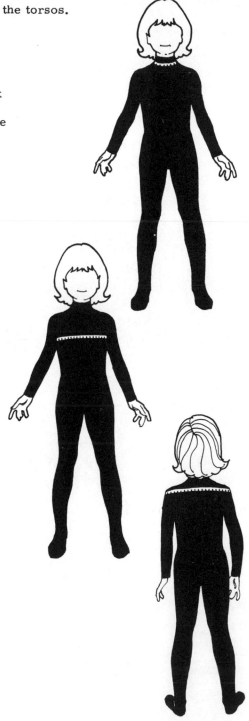

2. <u>Chest</u>. Measure around loosely from

   underarm to underarm add 2".

3. <u>Shoulder</u>. Measure across the back

   from shoulder to shoulder.

4. <u>Waist</u>. Children ages 1 through 6 years
   have no waist, so measure around the area
   in the position of the belly button to use as
   the waist measurement. From six years,
   measure the waist the same as for an adult.

5. <u>Skirt Length</u>. Measure from the waist to
   the desired length.

6. <u>Dress Length</u>. Measure from the back neck
   bone down to the back of the knee and subtract
   2".

7. <u>Back Waist Length.</u> Measure from the back
   neck to the waist.

8. <u>Front Waist Length.</u> Measure from the neck point over the chest and down to the waist.

9. <u>Short Sleeve Length.</u> Measure from the shoulder point down 6".

10. <u>Long Sleeve Length.</u> Bend the arm slightly measure from shoulder point down to the wrist bone.

11. <u>Hip</u>. The hip measurement is the same as the chest measurement plus 2".

12. <u>Shorts Length</u>. Measure from the waist down the desired length.

13. <u>Slacks Length.</u> Tie a string around the waist, measure from the waist or string down to the ankle bone.

14. <u>3/4 Sleeve.</u> Measure from shoulder point down

to the elbow, add 3".

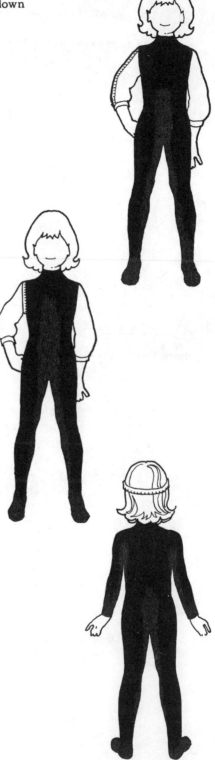

15. <u>Armhole.</u> Bend the arm slightly out to

the side, measure around the armhole,

add 2".

16. <u>Head.</u> Measure loosely around the head

about 1" above the eyebrows.

Children's Personal Measurement Chart

Part of Body	inch	cm *	Formulas inch	cm
1. Neck	13	32.5	N ÷ 6 = 2-1/8	5.4
2. Chest	30	75	C ÷ 4 = 7-1/2	18.8
3. Shoulder	13	32.5	S ÷ 2 = 6-1/2	16.2
4. Waist	25	62.5	W ÷ 4 = 6-1/4	15.6
5. Skirt Length	18	45		
6. Dress Length	34	85		
7. Back Waist Length	13	32.5		
8. Front Waist Length	13	32.5		
9. Short Sleeve Length	6	15		
10. Long Sleeve Length	18	45		
11. 3/4 Sleeve Length	13	32.5		
12. Hip	30	75	H ÷ 4 = 7-1/4	18.1
13. Armhole (sleeveless)	13	32.5	A.H. ÷ 2 =6-1/2	16.2
14. Armhole (with sleeves)	15	37.5	A.H.÷2 +2"=9-1/2	23.8
15. Head	21	52.5		
16. Shorts Length	13	32.5		
17. Slacks Length	34	85		

* cm means centimeters

Chart of Children's Measurements-Size 12

Part of body	inch	cm.
1. Neck		
2. Chest		
3. Shoulder		
4. Waist		
5. Skirt Length		
6. Dress Length		
7. Back Waist Length		
8. Front Waist Length		
9. Short Sleeve Length		
10. Long Sleeve Length		
11. 3/4 Sleeve Length		
12. Hip		
13. Shorts Length		
14. Armhole (sleeveless)		
15. Armhole (with sleeves)		
16. Slacks Length		
17. Head		

17

Children's Front & Back Torso

When drawing the right angle for the front torso, the
right angle should point toward the left. Draw a right
angle (⌐) line. The vertical line will be the center
front or fold line. The horizontal line will be the shoulder line. Make a mark over 6-1/2" on the horizontal
line for the shoulder point. To draw the neck opening,
follow this formula:

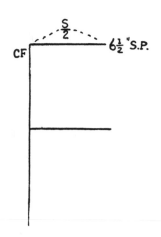

neck measurement divided by 6

(13 divided by 6 = 2-1/8 " + 3/4" = 2-7/8").

From the right angle corner, measure down on the
vertical line 2-7/8". Measure across on the horizontal
line 2-1/8". Make the neck curve by drawing a curved
line from the 2-7/8" point up to the 2-1/8" point.
The formula for determining the position of the bust
line is:

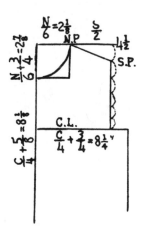

chest measurement divided by 4 + 5/8"

(30" divided by 4=7-1/2" + 5/8"=8-1/8'). Measure down
the center front line from the neck 8-1/8" and draw the
bust line.

The formula to determine the length of the bust line
is:

chest measurement divided by 4 + 3/4"

(30" divided by 4=7-1/2" + 3/4" = 8-1/4"). Draw the front
bust line 8-1/4" long. Divide the bust line into six
parts. Connect neck point with a straight line to the

Drawing the Front Torso (continued)

first division point.   This is the shoulder point.   At the fourth division, measure

in 3/8" and connect to the first division shoulder point with a curved line, con-

tinuing the line to the 5-1/2" division or bust line.   Measure down from the

shoulder point 13" for the back waistline.   Draw this line across the torso the

same length as the bust line.   Draw a straight line from the bust line 8-1/4"

down to the waistline and across the same length as the bust line.   Extend

the center front line 1/2" at the bottom.   Connect to the side waistline.

Children have no bust, but have a stomach so the front waistline is 1/2" longer

than the back waistline.

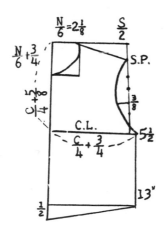

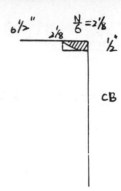

Draw a right angle pointing toward the right (⌐). The vertical line will be the center back line and the horizontal line
will be the basic shoulder line. To draw the shoulder follow
the formula:

shoulder length divided by 2

(13" divided by 2=6-1/2"). Make a mark over 6-1/2" from the right
angle for shoulder point. To draw the neck opening, follow the
formula: neck measurement divided by 6

(13" divided by 6=2-1/8"). Measure over from the right angle 2-1/8".

Measure down 1/2". Connect the 2-1/8" point to the 1/2"
point with a curved line to finish the neck opening. The back
chest line position is determined by this formula:

chest measurement divided by 4

(30" divided by 4=7-1/2"). The length of the chest line is
determined by the formula:

chest measurement divided by 4 + 3/4"

(30" divided by 4 = 7-1/2" + 3/4" = 8-1/4") Measure down from
the back neck (1/2" down from the right angle) 7-1/2". Draw a
line across the torso 8-1/4" long. Draw a straight line from
shoulder point to this chest line. Divide this line into 6 parts.
Connect the neck point with a straight line to the first division point.
This is shoulder point. At the third division, measure in 3/8". Connect with a curved line to shoulder point (first division) and continue
the curved line to the fifth division connecting to the 8-1/4" mark
at the chest line. Measure from the neck down the amount of the back
waist length (13"). Draw a line across the same length as the bust line for
waistline. Draw a straight line from the chest line (8-1/4") down to the
waistline.

18

Children's Sleeves

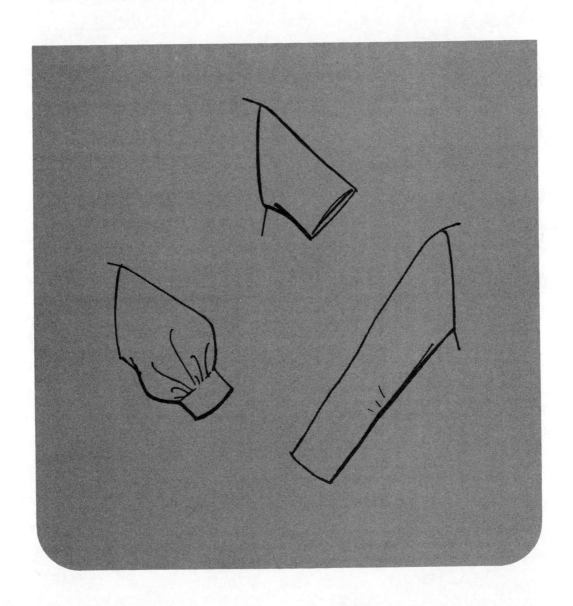

Using the measurements for a size 12, the long sleeve

length = 18", short sleeve length = 6", upper arm = 11"

armhole measurement with sleeves = armhole measure-

ment + 2" = 15".   The sleeve cap is determined by

the formula:

   armhole measurement divided by 4

(15" divided by 4 = 3-3/4").

Short Sleeve

A to B = armhole divided by 2 (15" divided by 2 =7-1/2")

A to D = armhole divided by 4 (15" divided by 4 = 3-3/4")

A to E = sleeve length = 6"

F to G = 11" upper arm measurement

Connect A B F G C A to complete drawing

Long Sleeve

To make the long sleeve follow the directions for the

short sleeve except make the length 18" long instead

of 6".   The formula for drawing the lower width of

the sleeve is:

   measure around the wrist tightly and add 2 divided by 2
   (wrist measurement + 2" divided by 2)

(6-1/2" + 2" = 8-1/2" divided by 2= 4-1/4").   From the 18"

sleeve length line, draw a line across 4-1/4".   Connect

with a straight line to the underarm point.

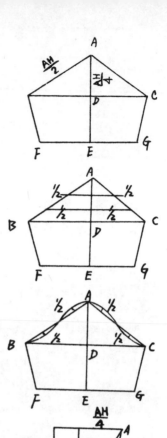

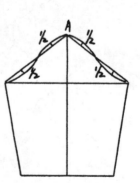

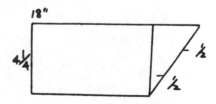

19

Girl's Clothes

Children's Dresses

All children's dresses are made with A-line style gathered or pleated skirts. Save 4" for the hem.

Simple Dress

Draw the front torso pattern according to the child's measurements. Extend the center front line the desired length. Extend the underarm line to match. Divide the dress bottom into two parts. Measure one section and extend the bottom the width of this one section. Connect to the armhole with a straight line. Measure up 1" from the bottom on the underarm edge. Connect with a curved line to the second section. Do not change the original torso neck or armhole.

Back

Draw the back torso.

Divide the skirt bottom into three parts.

Extend the bottom the width of one section.

Complete the drawing the same as the front.

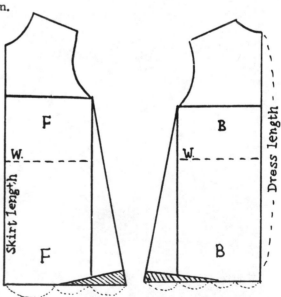

Jumper Dress for Children Ages 1 to 12

This style dress may be worn with a sweater or blouse. Draw a front torso. Measure from the neck down the center front 3". Measure from neck point over on the shoulder line 2". Connect these two points with a curved line.

Extend the center front the desired length. Extend the underarm line the same length.

Divide the dress bottom into three sections. Measure up from the skirt bottom on the underarm edge and connect to the second section. Extend the skirt bottom the width of one section. Do not change the armhole or neck of the original torso.

Back

Draw the back torso. Complete the same as the front. Draw the neck by measuring down from the neck on the center back 2" and connect to a point 2" across the shoulder from neck point.

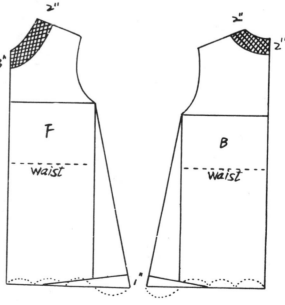

Gathered Yoke Style Dress

Make this style dress in paper, lay it on the fabric and cut.

Draw a front torso. Extend the center front the desired skirt length. Extend the bottom of the skirt 1" up 1/2" and connect to the armhole. Half way between neck point and bust line, draw a line across the torso. This line is the line used for the yoke. Cut on this line. When cutting fabric, add 1" seam on this line, 1" at shoulder, 1/2" around the armhole, 4" down the center front for extra material to gather. Add 4" on the skirt bottom for the hem, 1" on sides and 1" at top where the yoke was cut. To draw the front neck, measure down the center front from the neck 1" and across the shoulder line from shoulder point 1". Connect these two points with a curved line.

Back

Draw a back torso. There is no yoke in the back. Add desired length at the center front and underarm side. Extend the skirt bottom 1" up 1/2". Add 1" on center back if a zipper is used. If the back is to be buttoned , add 2". To draw the neck opening, measure down 1/2" on the center back from the neck. Measure across the shoulder line from neck point 1". Connect these two points with a curved line.

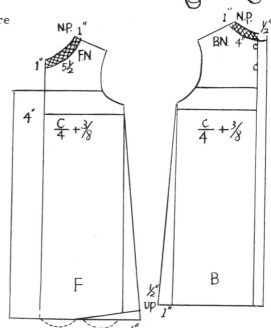

Collar

Children's collars are not cut on the fold of the material, but are cut as two sections.

After drawing the new neck, the measurement of the front neck is 11" and the back neck measurement is 8".

Using the formula, <u>F. N. +B. N. divided by 2</u> (11"+ 8" = 19" divided by 2=9-1/2").

Draw a right angle, measure up 2" and extend the line another 2".

Draw a line from the first 2" point to the opposite corner equal to 9-1/2".

Divide this line in half and draw a line in 1/2" long. Connect these points with a curved line. Measure up 2" from the left end of the length line. At the second extension point, measure in 1/2" and trim away the excess.

Connect this 1/2" point to the 2" point with a curved line.

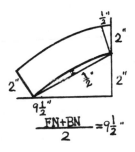

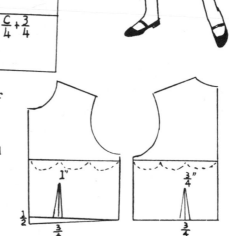

Draw a front torso.   Make no changes.

Dart

To draw the front dart, draw in the
chest line length using the formula:
C. divided by 4+3/4" (30" divided by
4=7-1/2" + 3/4" = 8-1/4").   To find
the position of the chest line, follow
the same formula, C divided by 4 + 3/4".
Divide the chest line into three parts.   At
first division point, measure down 1".
This is the dart point.   Draw a line
from this point to the waistline.   Measure over
3/8" on each side of this line and finish the
3/4" wide dart with two straight lines.   Extend
the center front 1/2" and connect to the
underarm side.

Back

Draw a back torso.   Make no changes except to add 3" down the center front for
buttons and fold-under.   Draw in the back chest line using the formula, C divided
by 4 + 3/4" , for the position and length of the line.

Dart

Make the back dart the same as the front dart except the dart point is 3/4"
down instead of 1" down as for the front.

Skirt for Gathered Style Dress

The width of the skirt top is determined by the formula, <u>waist measurement x 3.</u>

Using the measurements in the drawing the waist measurement is 25".

(25" x 3 = 75").

Draw the skirt 75" wide and 22" long (18" + 4" hem = 22").

Measure down the center back from the top of the skirt 6" add 3" for the

buttons and fold-under.

Before cutting, add 1/2" seams all around the skirt as well as the 4" hem.

Measure down 1/2" from the skirt top, sew two rows of stitching, gather to

equal the waist measurement.

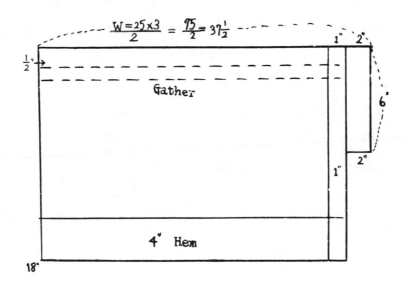

Shift Dress with a Ruffle at the Bottom

Draw a front torso. Extend the skirt length to measure 18"

long. To draw the neck opening, measure from the neck 3"

down the center front. Measure from shoulder point over 1-1/2"

on the shoulder line. Connect these two points with a curved

line to finish the neck. Extend the skirt bottom 1-1/2" up

1/2", connect to the armhole.

Back

Draw a back torso. Extend the skirt length 18". Extend the

skirt bottom 1-1/2" up 1/2", connect to the armhole.

Measure down the center back 2" from the neck. Measure

across the shoulder line 1-1/2" from neck point. Connect

these two points with a curve to finish the neck opening. Add

1" down the center back for the zipper.

Measure from the waist down 6" for the

zipper position.

Ruffle. Measure the skirt bottom times 3 to deter-

mine the length of the ruffle. Make the

ruffle 3" wide.

Hem the ruffle. Gather the top and sew to

the skirt bottom.

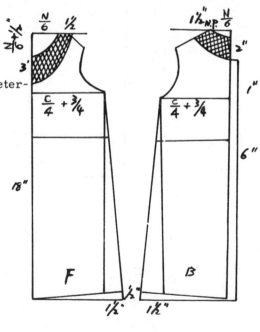

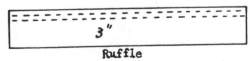

Ruffle

Basic School Dress with Yoke and Gathered Skirt

Draw a front torso. Extend the center front the
desired skirt length. Extend the bottom of the
skirt 1" up 1/2" and connect to the armhole.
Adjust the torso armhole 2" larger because this
dress has sleeves. Amhole 13" + 2" = 15".
Make the front armhole 7-1/2" around and the
back armhole 7-1/2" around. Draw the armhole
down 1" on the front and 1" down on the back.
No change in the neck. The yoke for this dress is
drawn on the chest line. Draw the chest line and
cut on this line. Add 1/2" seams all around
before cutting. Add 4" hem.

Back

Draw a back torso. Extend the center back
the same as the front. Extend the skirt
bottom 1" up 1/2" and connect to the armhole. Adjust the armhole. Cut on the chest
line, add seams.

Pocket

Make the pocket 6" long and 5" wide.
For the position of the pocket, measure
3" over from the center front on the waistline (or if the 4" addition is included in the
measurement the pocket will be 7" across).
Measure down 3/4" from the waistline on
the opposite side of the pocket, connect to

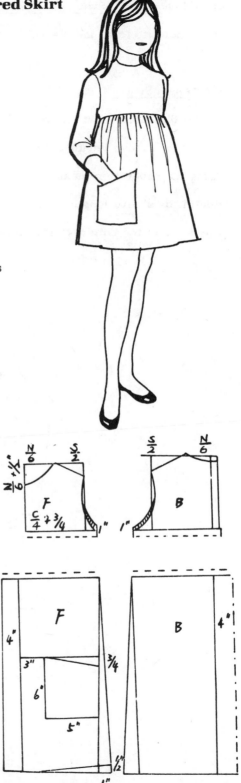

the 3" point to form the slant.

3/4 Length Sleeve

Follow the basic short sleeve directions.

Extend the sleeve length 13" (length of 3/4 sleeve).

Using the upper arm measurement of 11", draw the sleeve 5-1/2" wide each

side of the sleeve length line.

The width of the bottom of the sleeve must equal the upper arm measurement.

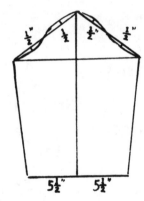

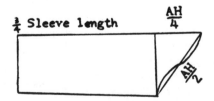

Dress with Peter Pan Collar and Front Pleat

Draw a front torso. Make no changes in the neck. Add 4" down the center front for the pleat. Adjust the armhole for sleeves (13" + 2" = 15"). Measure down 1" at the armhole edge and connect to the armhole. Draw the waistline from the original torso. Stitch the center front down to the waistline to form the pleat.

Back

Draw a back torso. Follow the same directions as the front. Add 1" down the center back for the zipper. Measure down 4" from the waist for the zipper position.

Collar

To determine the collar length line use the formula, <u>neck measurement divided by 2</u> (13" divided by 2=6-1/2"). Draw a right angle, measure up 2-1/2", extend the line 1-1/2". Draw the length line 6-1/2". From the first 2-1/2" extension draw a straight line 1-1/4" long.

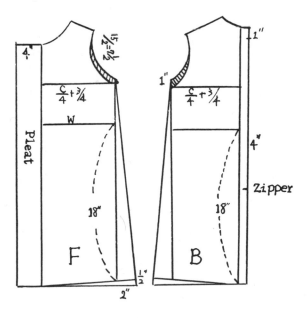

Dress with Peter Pan Collar and Front Pleat (continued)

Divide the line in half, and at this point

measure in 3/8" to draw the curve.

Extend the length line at a right angle

1-1/4" long.

Connect to the 1-1/2" point.

To round the collar corner, measure

in 1/2" and join to the collar length

line with a curve.

Sleeves

Follow basic short sleeve directions.

Tie

Draw a tie 1-1/2" wide and 20" long.

The tie will be 1/2" wide when finished.

Fold, sew raw edges, turn.

Tie in a bow and sew to the top of

the pleat.

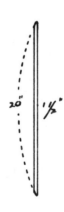

Honeycomb smocking provides a new custom touch for clothes, accessories and furnishings. It is the new use for an old fashioned stitch that gives it a smart, decorative appearance. If used on a solid-colored material, a smocking design is drawn on the fabric, and the smocking is worked on the right side of the fabric over straight rows of evenly spaced dots stamped about 1/4" apart to affect a half inch deep honeycomb shape, or with dots about 1/2" apart to produce a deeper design. Provide one yard of width for each half yard of finished smocking. The stitch itself is not difficult and can be easily learned by a novice following these few simple instructions:

1. Start the first row of smocking from right to left. The numbered diagram shows where to start smocking rows. The curved lines on the diagram show where dots are picked up to form stitches.

2. Pick up the first and second dots of the first row and draw the two dots together firmly, making an over-stitch.

3. Slip the needle through to the wrong side of the fabric and up through the next dot to the left, keeping the thread flat and make a second over-stitch.

4. Repeat to the end of the row always drawing two dots together to form one finished smocking dot and always holding the thread flat between smocked dots with your thumb.

The second row is worked over alternate dots to form the diamond honeycomb shape, and the pattern of the first and second rows is repeated until the entire section to be smocked is completed.

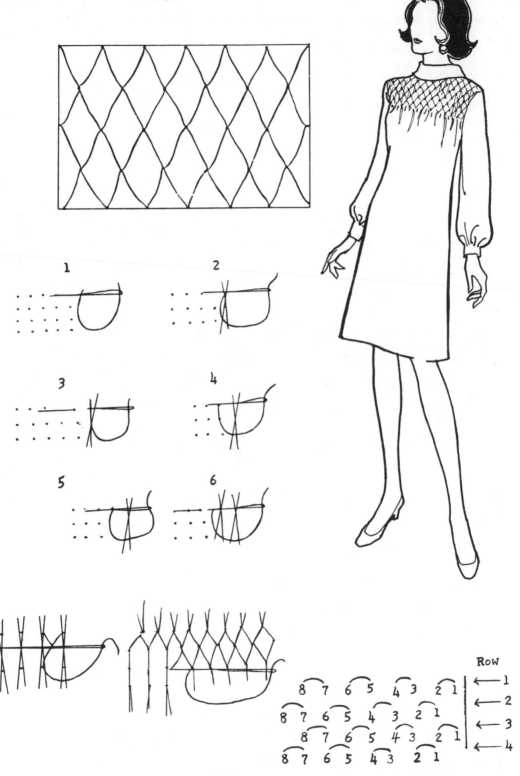

1

2

3

4

5

6

Row

← 1

← 2

← 3

← 4

8 7 6 5 4 3 2 1

Smocking on Plain Material

When smocking on plain material, draw a line 1" down from the top of the material. Draw additional vertical lines 3/4" apart for 13 rows. Draw horizontal lines 3/4" apart forming squares equal to the individual bust width measurement.

Smocking on Checked Material

Follow the checks in the material for guidelines for smocking checked material. Start smocking 1" down from the top of the fabric.

Child's Smocked Dress, Ages 1 to 12 years

Following the chest formula, chest measurement divided by 4 plus 2, smock the amount equal to this chest measurement. (36" divided by 4 + 2 = 11")

Use the formula, chest measurement divided by 4 + 1, to determine the width of the chest line (30" divided by 4 = 9 + 1 = 10"). This measurement is figured on the fold. After the material is smocked, it must measure 20".

Draw a front torso. Measure down the center front from the neck 1". Measure from neck point over on the shoulder line 1". Connect these two measurements with a curved line to make the neck opening.

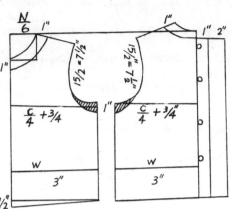

Extend the torso bottom 3", and add 3" down the center front.

Change the armhole to measure 15" (with sleeves) by measuring down 1" at the under-arm. Connect to the armhole.

Draw in the bust line following the formula,

<u>chest measurement divided by 4 + 3/4"</u>

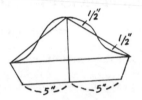

Back

Draw a back torso. Measure down the center front 1" from the neck. Measure across the shoulder line from neck point 1". Connect these two points to make the neck opening.

Make armhole changes the same as the front.

Sleeve

Draw a short sleeve following the directions on page 192.

Pleated Skirt

Draw a square equal to the <u>waist measurement x 3</u>

(25" x 3 = 75") and the skirt length (18") plus 3"

for hem.

>   <u>Amount of fabric necessary - waist measurement</u>
>
>   <u>= amount left for pleats</u> (25" x 3 = 75" - 25" = 50")

Always make 16 pleats in every skirt.

The formula to follow for figuring the width

of the outside pleat is:

>   <u>waist measurement divided by 16</u>
>
>   (25" divided by 16 = 1-1/2").

The formula to follow for figuring the width

of the inside pleat is:

>   <u>amount of fabric left for pleats divided by</u>
>
>   <u>16</u> (50" divided by 16 = 3").

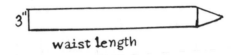

waist length

Waist = 25"

Outside pleat = 1-1/2"

Inside pleat = 3"

<u>Skirt Band</u>

Draw the skirt band equal to the

<u>waist measurement divided by 2.</u>

Draw the band 3" wide.

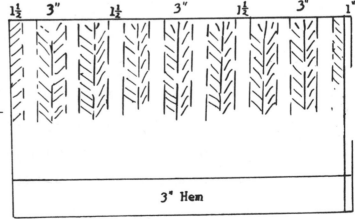

3" Hem

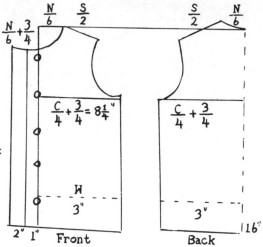

Draw a front torso. No changes are made in the neck. Adjust the armhole 2" larger for sleeves.

Draw in the chest line following the formula:

chest measurement divided by 4 + 3/4"

(30" divided by 4 + 3/4" = 8-1/4").

Add 3" down the center front for buttons and fold-under.

Buttons

Measure down the center front from the neck 1/2" for the position of the first button. Remaining buttons are 5" apart.

Back

Draw a back torso. Make no changes in the neck, but add 3" to the bottom of the torso. Adjust the armhole 2" larger for sleeves.

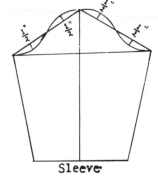

Sleeve

Sleeve

Follow directions for child's 3/4 length sleeve on page 192.

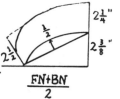

Collar

Draw a right angle. Measure up 2-3/8", extend 2-3/4". Using the formula, front neck measurement + back neck measurement divided by 2, draw a straight line from the 2-3/8" point equal to this length. At the end of the length line, draw another right angle 2-1/2" long. Connect to the 2-3/4" extension. Divide the straight line drawn from the 2-3/8" point in half and measure in 1/2" to form the curve for the neck.

To round the collar corner, measure in 1/2" at the collar point.

Skirt with Center Front Pleat

To draw the skirt front, draw a line for the waist using the formula:

<u>waist divided by 4 + 1"</u>

(25" divided by 4 + 1" = 7-1/4")

Draw the desired length line (13" + 3"= 16").

Add 3" down the center front for pleat.

Draw in the hip line using the formula:

<u>hip divided by 4 + 1"</u>

(30" divided by 4 = 7-1/2" + 1"= 8-1/2").

Skirt Back

To draw the skirt back, draw a line for the waist using the formula:

<u>waist divided by 4 + 2" (for elastic)</u>

(25" divided by 4 + 2" = 8-1/4")

Draw in the hip line following the formula:

<u>hip divided by 4 + 1"</u>

(30" divided by 4 + 1" = 8-1/2")

Skirt Band

Draw a line equal to the <u>waist measurement divided by 2 plus 3"</u> (front and back) for the skirt band length. Make the band 3" wide. The finished band will be 1" wide.

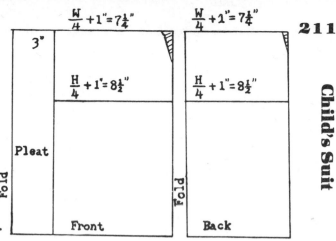

In the diagram:
- Left panel (Front): $\frac{W}{4}+1"=7\frac{1}{4}"$, 3", Fold, Pleat, $\frac{H}{4}+1"=8\frac{1}{2}"$, Front
- Right panel (Back): $\frac{W}{4}+1"=7\frac{1}{4}"$, Fold, $\frac{H}{4}+1"=8\frac{1}{2}"$, Back

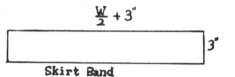

$\frac{W}{2}+3"$

3"

Skirt Band

Draw a front torso. Extend the center front the desired coat length. Add a total of 5-1/2" down the center front (2-1/2" for double breasted lap and 3" for fold-under).

To draw the neck, measure down the center front 3/4" from the neck. Measure from neck point across the shoulder 1/2". Connect these two points with a curved line to form the neck opening.

Armhole

Measure down 1-1/2" from the underarm and connect to the armhole with a curved line.

Extend the skirt bottom 2" up 1/2". Connect with a straight line to the underarm. Draw in the chest line using the formula:

chest measurement divided by 4 + 2" (30" divided by 4 + 2"= 9-1/2")

Pocket

Measure down 2-3/4" on the center front from the waistline. Draw a line across the torso for the pocket position. Make the pocket 5" wide from the underarm side, and 5-1/2" long. To make the pocket round at the corner, measure in 1".

Buttons (6)

Measure down the center front 1-1/2" for the position of the first button. Place each remaining button 5" apart.

Back

Draw a back torso. Measure from neck point across the shoulder line 1/2". Connect to the center back neck with a curved line to form the neck opening. Lower the armhole 1-1/2" as was done for the front. Draw in the bust line the same as the front.

Extend the skirt bottom 1-3/4" up 1/2". Connect to the underarm with a

straight line.

<u>Collar</u>

Draw a right angle. Measure up 3-1/2", extend the line 4-1/2" long.

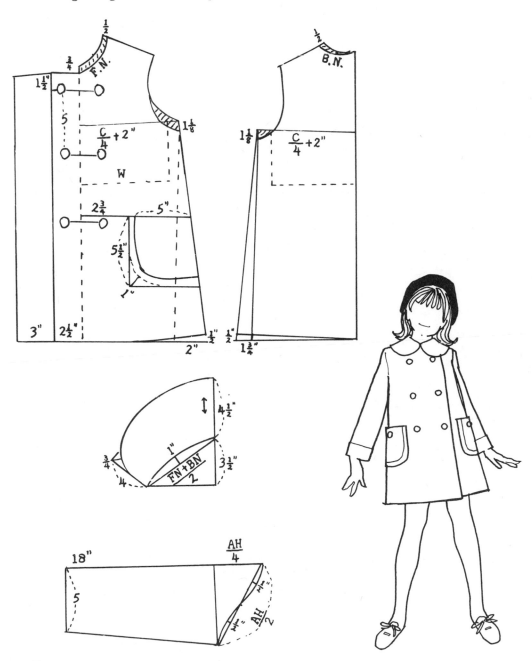

Child's Coat (continued)

Using the formula,

front neck + back neck divided by 2

draw a straight line from the 3-1/2" point equal to the collar length. Divide
this line in half, and at this point measure in 1". Make the neck curve by
connecting the 3-1/2" point to the length line touching the 1" in point at the
half measurement. Draw another right angle at the end of the length line
4" long. Connect to the 4-1/2" extension. To round the collar corner,
measure in 3/4" at the collar point. Connect to the 4-1/2" point.

Long Sleeve

Refer to the directions for the child's long sleeve on page 192.

Cutting

Before cutting the fabric, be sure to save 1/2" at the neck and armhole
for seams as well as 1" on the side.

Lining

For the coat front lining, copy the coat front, but do not include the 3" added
down the center front. For seams add 1/2" at the neck and armhole, 1" on
the side and 3" for the hem.

For the coat back lining, copy the coat back adding 1/2" at the neck and
armhole, 1" at the sides as well as 3" for the hem.

Children ages 1 to 12 will enjoy wearing these comfortable pajamas while relaxing.

Draw a front torso. No changes will be made in the neck. Draw the bust line using previously learned formula. Add 2" down the center front for Chinese Frogs and fold-under. Add 2" to the torso bottom and measure in 2" on each side of torso bottom to make the coat round.

Back

Draw the back torso. Follow the same directions as the front.

Pants

Follow directions for the Bermuda Shorts. Draw the shorts front by measuring up 3" on the hip side and 1" across on the bottom. Connect these two points with a curved line to form the rounded pants bottom. Draw the pants bottom 3" each side of the crease line.

Draw the shorts back following the shorts front drawing. Make the shorts bottom 3-1/2" each side of the crease line. Add 1-1/2" to the top of the front and back pants for the casing. Insert elastic through the casing to equal the waist measurement.

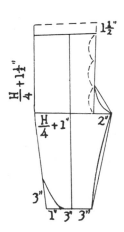

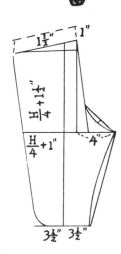

Collar for Chinese Lounging Pajamas

Draw a right angle. Measure up 1", draw the length line (N divided by 2 = 6-1/2"). Make a square by connecting the 1" measurement to the 6-1/2" measurement. To form the collar points, measure up 1/2" and 3/4" across the top. Connect the 3/4" point to the 1/2" point. Finally connect to the 6-1/2" point.

Collar

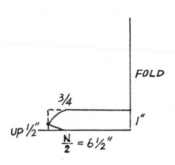

Pajamas

No side seams are made in these pajamas, so the torso is drawn on the fabric with the hip side placed on the fold.

In the drawings, the dark line represents the front and the dotted line is the back.

To draw the front, draw the length of the slacks (38"). Follow the formula, hip measurement divided by 4+ 1-1/2" (38" divided by 4 + 1-1/2"= 11"), to draw the crotch line.

Follow the formula, hip measurement divided by 4 + 1 (38" divided by 4 + 1 = 10-1/2") to draw the length of the crotch line. Make the square the same as made when drawing the slacks. Extend the crotch line 2" at the crotch. Measure up 4" from the crotch line, connect the 2" extension to this 4" measurement with a curved

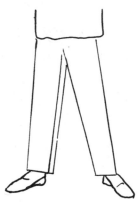

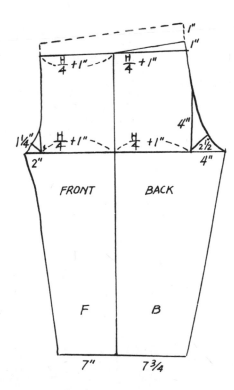

Pajamas (continued)

line. Make the pajamas 7" wide at the bottom and connect to the 2" extension at the crotch with a curved ruler. This 7" is always the width of the pajama leg for children regardless of size.

Back

Study the dotted lines in the illustration. Measure over on the waistline 1" in and extend 1". Connect to the center back.

At the crotch extend 2" and measure down 1/2". Make a mark 1-1/4" out from the original square made when drawing the pajamas. Connect the 2" extension (down 1/2" point) touch the 1-1/4" point with a curved line to the 1" extension at the waist.

Extend the pajama bottom 3/4" on the crotch side. Connect to the crotch with a curved line.

Add 1" at the waistline before cutting.

This 1" is turned under to form a

casing for elastic.

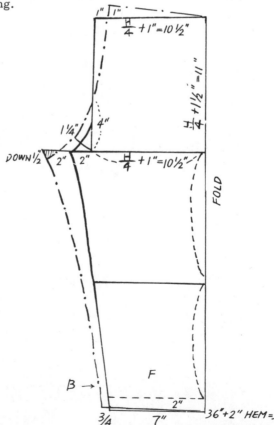

20

Men's & Boy's Clothes

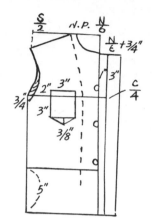

Draw a front torso using the children's measurement directions. Add 4" down the center front (1" for buttons and 3" for fold-under). Extend the center front length 5" for a tuck-in shirt. Extend the center front 3" for a shirt worn outside the pants. No changes are made in the neck. This shirt has sleeves so it is necessary to draw the armhole equal to the armhole measurement plus 2" (13" + 2" = 15").

Measure down 3/4" at the armhole and connect this measurement to the remaining armhole curve. The position of the chest line is determined by the formula:

<u>chest measurement divided by 4</u>

(30" divided by 4 = 7-1/2").

To determine the length of the chest line follow the formula:

<u>chest measurement divided by 4 + 3/4"</u>

(30" divided by 4 + 3/4" = 8-1/4").

Measure down 7-1/2" from neck point and draw a line 8-1/4" across the torso.

Position of the Pocket

Measure down from the original torso center front over 2". Draw the pocket 3" wide and 2-3/4" long. Divide the bottom of the pocket in half. At this half point, draw a line down 3/8". Connect this 3/8" point to each edge of the pocket with straight lines to form a point at the bottom of the pocket.

Back

Draw a back torso. No changes are made in the neck. Change the armhole the same as the front. Measure down 3/4". Connect to the remaining armhole curve. Extend the center back length 5". Draw the chest line following the same formulas and directions used for the front.

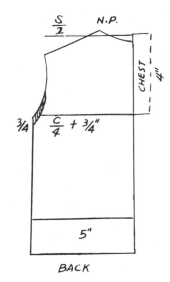

BACK

Collar

Study the drawing. Using the formula, <u>neck measurement divided by 2</u> (13" divided by 2 = 6-1/2"), draw a line 6-1/2" long. Add a right angle line 2-1/4" long. Make a square by drawing a line across the top 6-1/2" long and another line 2-1/4" down. Divide the collar into three equal parts. Extend the top collar line 3/4". Measure up 3/8" at the bottom of the third division, connect to the 3/4" extension. Finally connect the 3/8" point to the second division.

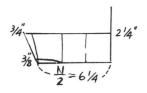

Sleeves

Follow the children's short sleeve directions on page 192 except use the formula , <u>armhole divided by 6</u>, to determine the sleeve cap (A to D in the picture). Follow this sleeve cap formula when drawing a boy's sleeve. To complete the sleeve, measure up 3/8" at the bottom of the upper arm, connect to the armhole so sleeve will not be too wide.

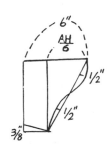

Boxer Shorts for Boys

To draw the shorts, draw a vertical line the
length of the shorts.

To determine the position of the crotch line
follow the formula,

hip measurement divided by 4 + 2"

To determine the length of the crotch line
follow the formula,

hip measurement divided by 4 + 1"

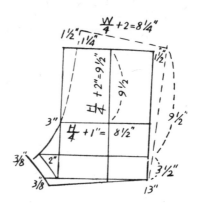

Using the measurements in the children's chart,
the hip = 30" divided by 4 + 2" = 9-1/2".

Draw a vertical line 9-1/2", and draw
a horizontal line 8-1/2" long (30" divided by 4
+ 1" = 8-1/2").   Add straight lines on each side, top, and bottom to
form a square.   Extend the left side of the crotch line 2-1/8".

Measure up on the square 3".   Connect the 3" point to the 2-1/8" extension.

Connect the 2-1/8" point with a curved line to the shorts bottom line.

Add 1/2" seams at the waistline, and on both sides of the shorts, 1-1/2"
for hem and cut.

Back

The dotted lines in the drawing indicate the shorts back.

Lay the front shorts on the fabric, and make the following changes:

1.   On the crotch side of the waistline measure over 1-1/2"
     up 1-1/4".   Study the dotted lines in the drawing.

2.   Use the formula, waist measurement divided by 4 + 2".

to determine the waist length line (25" divided by 4 + 2" = 8-1/4").

Draw a straight line from the 1-1/2" point 8-1/4" long.

3. Connect the 1-1/2" point to the crotch with a curved line.

4. Extend the crotch line on the left 2", down 3/8" and connect
    to the remaining crotch with a curved line.

5. Connect the 8-1/4" point to the shorts bottom or length line.

6. Add 1/2" seams at the waistline and on both sides of the
    shorts. Add 1-1/2" at the bottom for hem.

Facing

Because these shorts have elastic at the top, make a facing. To

determine the length of the facing follow the formula,

waist measurement divided by 4 + 2" x 4

Using the measurements in the chart, waist = 25" divided by 4 + 2

x 4 = 33". Cut a facing 1-1/2" wide and 33" long.

The length of the elastic should equal the waist measurement.

Sew the casing to the shorts top for a casing. Insert the elastic in the casing.

Boys Long Elasticized Pants

Make these long pants following the instructions

for boxer shorts and add the desired length to

inside and outside edges of shorts drawing.

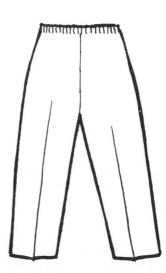

Study the illustration carefully, the left side is the overalls front and the right side is the overalls back. Draw a vertical line to equal the overalls length. To determine the position of the crotch line follow the formula:

chest measurement divided by 4 + 3-1/4"

To determine the length of the crotch line follow the formula:

chest measurement divided by 4 + 1-1/4"

The length of the slacks in the drawing is 24".

Draw a vertical line 24" long.

Chest measurement in the drawing is 24"

(24" divided by 4 + 3-1/4" = 9-1/4").

Draw a horizontal line 9-1/4" down from the top of the vertical line.

Chest measurement = 24" divided by 4 + 1-1/4" = 7-1/4".

Draw a horizontal line 7-1/4" long on each side of the vertical line.

Draw a square by connecting the existing lines as directed for slacks or shorts.

On the right side of the crotch line, extend the line 2-3/4". At the right top of the overalls extend the line up 1". Connect the 1" point to the 2-3/4" crotch point with a straight line. Divide this line in half. At the half mark, draw a line in 5/8". Connect the 1" point to the 2-3/4" point touching the 5/8" point with a curved line.

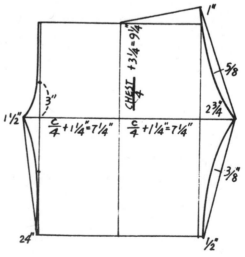

Extend the square 1/2" on the right side at the bottom. Connect the 1/2"
extension to the 2-3/4" point at the crotch with a straight line. Divide this line
in half. At the half point draw a line in 3/8". Connect the 2-3/4" point,
touch the 3/8" point to the 1/2" extension at the bottom with a curved line to
finish the crotch. This section is the overalls back.

To draw the overalls front, extend the 7-1/4" crotch line 1-1/2" on the left
side of the picture. Measure up 3" on the square and connect the 3" point to
the 1-1/2" crotch point with a straight line. Draw a straight line from the
1-1/2" crotch point to the overalls length line. Divide this length line in
half. Connect this half point to the 1-1/2" extension.

Back Facing for the Elastic

Elastic is inserted in the back of the overalls, for this reason sew a facing
to the overalls back.

To make the facing length for the elastic use the formula:

> chest measurement divided by 4 + 1-1/4" x 2

> (24" divided by 4 + 1-1/4" x 2 = 14-1/2")

Draw a square 14-1/2" long and 1-1/2" wide. Sew to the overalls
back. Cut the elastic length following the formula:

> waist measurement divided by 2

> (22" divided by 2 = 11").

Cut the elastic 11" long. Insert in the casing.

Bib

Draw a square 5-1/2" long by 2-1/2" wide at the top by 3"
wide at the bottom. Cut two, adding seam allowance of
1/2" all around the edges. Sew around three edges and

BIB

sew this bib to the overalls top by matching the fold of the bib to the center front waistline. Make a buttonhole on each corner of the bib 1/2" down from the top, and 1/2" in at the side.

<u>Strap</u>

Draw a rectangle 1-1/4" wide and 12" long. Divide one end of the strap in half. At the half point, draw a line out 1/2". Connect to the ends of the strap to form a point. Sew button on the point. As the child grows, the button may be moved down the strap.

Make two straps, cross them in the back and sew to the overalls back.

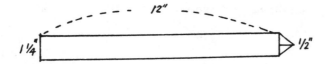

The following measurements are used in the sport shirt and bathrobe descriptions:

1. <u>Chest</u>. Measure around the chest from underarm to underarm. Add 4". 44" was used in the drawing.

2. <u>Shoulder</u>. Place two rulers upright on the arms at the shoulder position. Measure from ruler to ruler across the back (20").

3. <u>Front waist length.</u> Measure from neck to waist (22").

4. <u>Upperarm.</u> Measure around the largest part of the arm (13").

5. <u>Armhole.</u> Measure around the armhole. Add 2". (19" + 2" = 21").

6. <u>Short sleeve length.</u> Desired length (9")

7. <u>Long sleeve length.</u> Desired length (25")

8. <u>Sport shirt length.</u> Desired length from neck (30")

9. Bathrobe length. Desired length from neck (46")

Men's Sport Shirt

Before marking on the fabric allow enough fabric at the top to equal the back neck measurement (3-3/4").

The formula, <u>men's chest measurement divided by 12</u>, is the amount to mark across for the neck opening (44" divided by 12 = 3-3/4").

Draw a right angle (⌐).

Men's Sport Shirt (continued)

Measure across the horizontal line 3-3/4" (this is neck point). Measure down the vertical line 3-3/4". Connect these two points with a curved line to form the neck opening.

To mark the shoulder, measure from neck point across the line using the formula,

shoulder divided by 2

20" divided by 2 = 10". At this point, measure down 1-3/4", connect this 1-3/4" point to neck point with a straight line.

Draw the center front line down from the neck to the desired length (30").

Draw the front width line using the formula,

chest divided by 6

44" divided by 6 = 7-3/8". Draw the front width line 7-3/8" down from neck point. Draw a straight line down from the shoulder point. The front width line ends at this line drawn from shoulder point. Draw the chest line using the formula,

chest measurement divided by 4 + 2"

44" divided by 4 + 2" = 13". Draw the chest line 13" down from neck point. Touch the end of the line drawn from shoulder point. Draw the armhole starting at the shoulder point, touch the front width line and curve down to the chest line. Measure the armhole. It must equal the armhole measurement divided by 2 + 2".

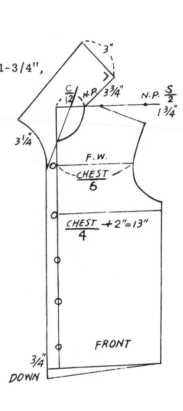

Draw a straight line down from the armhole the length of the sport shirt, and connect to the center front length line.

Extend the center front 1" for buttons.

At the center front bottom, measure down 3/4" and connect with a straight line to the underarm.

If a slit is desired on the side of the sport shirt, leave the right side open 2-1/4".

Pocket

Measure 2" over from the center front on the chest line for the pocket position. Make the pocket 4-1/2" wide and 5" long.

Buttons

The position of the first button is on the front width line at the center front line. Remaining buttons are 3" apart.

Collar

The collar is drawn on the existing shirt in the following manner:

at the neck point draw a right angle line up to equal the back

neck measurement or chest measurement (44" divided by 12

= 3-3/4"). From the top of this measurement draw a line across 3",

which is the width of the collar. At the center front extension draw a right

angle line 3-1/4" long. Connect to the top of the collar.

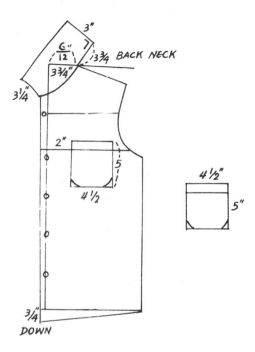

Men's Sport Shirt Collar (continued)

Add 1" seam allowance on the side of the shirt, 1/2" at the armhole, 1" at the shoulder, 1/2" around the collar, 1/2" down the center front, and 2" at the bottom for the hem. Cut out the shirt.

Facing for the collar

Lay the front shirt on the fabric, draw around the collar and down the center front. Make this facing 3" wide beginning at the front width line. Make the width 3" all along the length of the center front line.

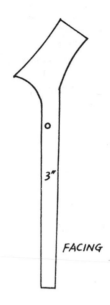

Back of sport shirt

Draw a right angle (⌐). Measure across the horizontal line the amount equal to the chest measurement divided by 12 (44" divided by 12 = 3-3/4"). Extend this mark up 3/4". Mark the shoulder point by using the formula:

   shoulder divided by 2

(20" divided by 2 = 10"). Make a mark 10" across the line. Measure from this point down 1-1/4". Connect this 1-1/4" point to the 3/4" extension

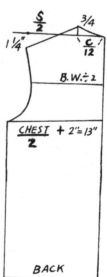

with a straight line. Draw in the front width line, chest line, and armhole the same as the front using the same formulas. Draw the center back line the same length as the center front line. Draw the underarm line the same and connect across the bottom to the center back.

The sleeve cap is determined by the

formula:

armhole divided by 6

(21" divided by 6 = 3-1/2").

A to D = 3-1/2"

A to B = armhole measurement divided by 2

= 10-1/2"

A to E = 9" short sleeve length.

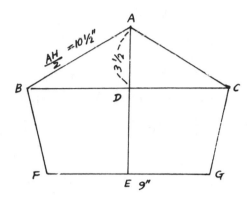

To draw the sleeve curve, divide the sleeve

at armhole edge in three parts. Divide the

first section in half and make a mark out 1/2".

Divide the second section in half and make a

mark in 1/2". Connect the points to form the

sleeve curve. This is the sleeve front.

Draw the front sleeve first.

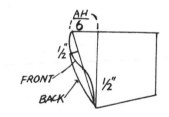

To draw the back sleeve, connect the underarm

point to the first 1/2" mark with a straight

line instead of a curved line.

When cutting the fabric allow 1/2" seam

allowance and 2" hem.

Cut the back sleeve section first.

Open the fabric and cut the other side with

the curve which would be the front sleeve.

Men's Bathrobe

Refer to the measurements given for the sport shirt to draw the men's bathrobe. Study the accompanying drawing carefully. To draw the back neck of the bathrobe draw a right angle (⌐). Mark neck point by measuring across the horizontal line using the formula:

chest measurement divided by 4 + 3/8"

(44" divided by 4 + 3/8" = 11-3/8"). Measure down the vertical line 1-1/4". Connect the 1-1/4" to the neck point with a curved line. This is the back neck. Draw the center front the desired length. Measure across the basic shoulder line using the formula, shoulder divided by 2 (20" divided by 2 = 10"). Measure down 1-3/4", connect the 1-3/4" point to neck point with a straight line. Draw a straight line from the basic shoulder line down to equal the measurement, chest divided by 4 (44" divided by 4 = 11").

Draw the chest line across the bathrobe using the formula:

chest divided by 4 + 1"

(44" divided by 4 + 1" = 12"). Starting at center front draw a line across the bathrobe 12" long. Draw in the armhole starting at shoulder point, touch the line drawn from the basic shoulder line, and curve to the chest line.

Connect the underarm to the length line and draw a line across the bottom to connect to the center front length.

Extend the bottom right side of the bathrobe 1". Connect the 1" extension to the underarm. Measure up 3/4" on the center front bottom, connect to the 1" extension on the other side of the bathrobe.

Front Neck

Make another drawing exactly like the one just finished, except change the neck for the front as follows:

Measure down 2-1/2" from the chest line, connect this point to neck point with a straight line.

Before cutting, add 1" at shoulder, 1" along the side, 1" down the center front, 1/2" around the neck for seam allowances and 3"for hem.

Pocket

Draw a line across the bathrobe down from the basic shoulder line equal to the front waist length measurement (22"). Draw the line across the bathrobe to the underarm side. Draw the pocket 3" down from the front waist length line. Make the pocket 6-1/4" wide and 7-1/2" long. If a round pocket is desired instead of a square, just draw the corners of the pocket round at the bottom.

Trimming down the center front

Draw the same length as the robe. Extend the center front the length of the formula, <u>chest measurement divided by 12</u> (44" divided by 12 = 3-3/4") or the back neck measurement. Make the trimming 3-1/2" wide. Turn under 1/2" seams on both edges, fold and sew all around the bathrobe. The finished trim will be 1-3/4" wide.

Sleeves

Follow the same directions used for the short sleeve except extend the length of the sleeve the desired length (25") and when drawing the sleeve curve divide the line into three sections. On the half mark of the first division draw the line out 3/4" and in 1/4" at the half point of the second division. Measure in 1-1/4" at the sleeve bottom underarm side. Connect the 1-1/4" point to the underarm with a straight line.

Belt

Draw a belt 60" long and 4" wide. Place two edges together, sew along the edges and across the end, turn, sew end by hand.

Men's Bathrobe Diagramed

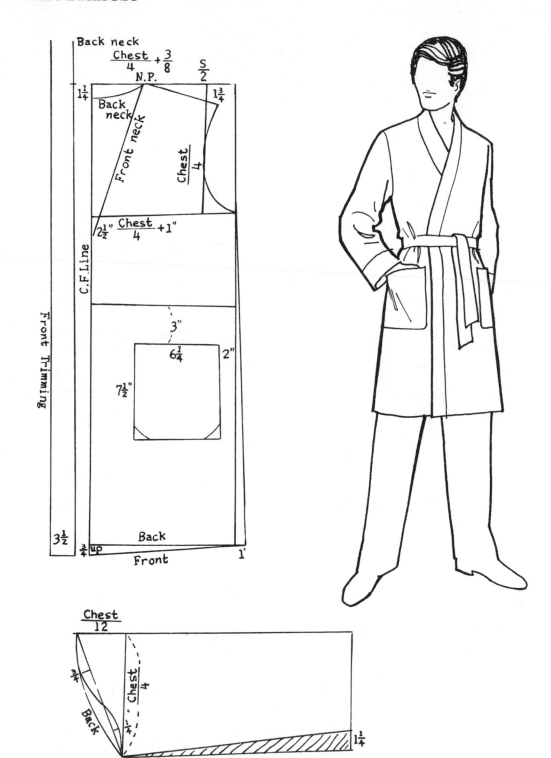

Back neck

$\dfrac{Chest}{4} + \dfrac{3}{8}$

N.P.

$\dfrac{S}{2}$

$1\frac{1}{4}$

$1\frac{3}{4}$

Back neck

Front neck

$\dfrac{Chest}{4}$

$2\frac{1}{2}$"　$\dfrac{Chest}{4} + 1$"

C.F. Line

Front Trimming

3"

$6\frac{1}{4}$

2"

$7\frac{1}{2}$"

$3\frac{1}{2}$

$\frac{3}{4}$ up

Back

Front

1'

$\dfrac{Chest}{12}$

$\frac{3}{4}$

$\dfrac{Chest}{4}$

$\frac{1}{4}$

Back

$1\frac{1}{4}$

In drawing the pattern, when the armhole is connected to the waist the inward curve of the ruler is used by placing the large end of the ruler at the armhole point.

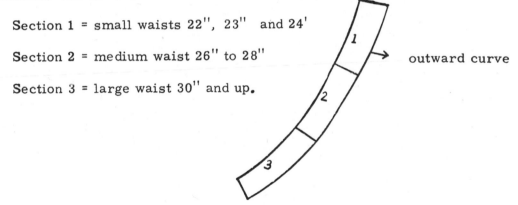

outward   inward curve

To connect the waistline to the hip point (8" down) divide the ruler into 3 equal sections, and use the outward curve as follows:

    Section 1 = small waists 22", 23" and 24'

    Section 2 = medium waist 26" to 28"

    Section 3 = large waist 30" and up.

outward curve

It is not necessary to have the curved ruler. However, it may make drawing curves easier. Many designers draw their own curves freehand.

21

Additional Sleeve Designs

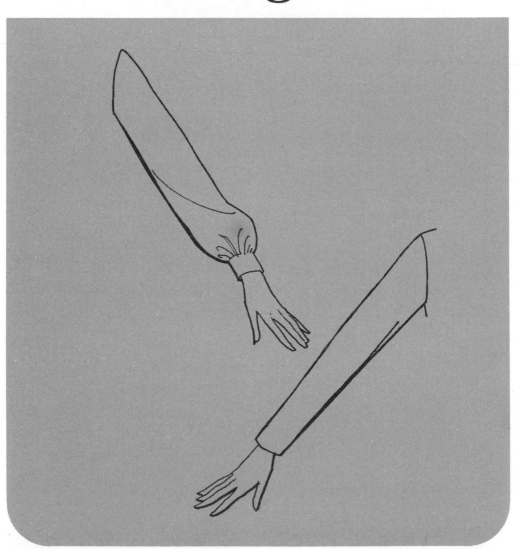

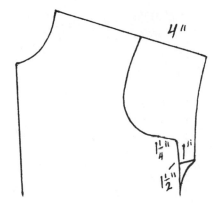

Front

Extend the shoulder line 4". Measure down 1-1/4" from underarm point then measure out 1". Draw a line from shoulder extension to the 1" mark, curve this line. Below the 1" extension draw a curved line 1-1/2" down from the 1" mark.

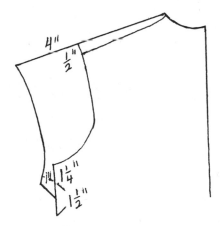

Back

Raise the back shoulder point 1/2" as illustrated and extend the shoulder line 4" as done on the front. Finish the diagram to match the front.

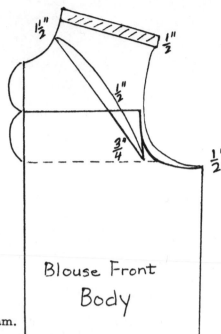

Blouse Front
Body

1.   Trim 1/2" off shoulder seam.

2.   Mark a line under arm.

3.   Divide it into two equal sections along center front.

4.   Square underarm and center of two equal sections at armhole.

5.   Measure up 3/4" on the underarm squared line.

6.   Measure down from the shoulder 1-1/2" at neck and connect

     this mark to the 3/4" mark.

7.   Find the center of the line, mark out 1/2" and curve.

8.   Mark down 1/2" at underarm and finish the sleeve line.

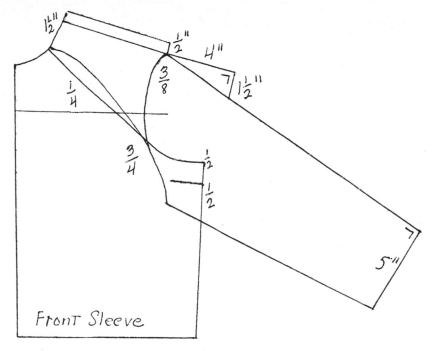

Front Sleeve

1. Trim off 1/2" at shoulder seam.

2. Mark a line under the arm.

3. Divide it into two equal parts.

4. Square underarm and center of two equal sections at underarm.

5. Measure up 3/4" on the underarm line.

6. Measure down neck 1-1/2". Connect to the underarm mark (3/4").

7. Find the center of the line and mark 1/4" out and curve to the
   3/4" line.

8. Measure and mark two 1/2" marks at underarm. On the second 1/2"
   mark measure in 2" and connect to 3/4" mark.

9. Mark 3/8" out on the shoulder line and extend the line 4" out and
   draw a line at right angle 1-1/2" down.

10. From the 3/8" mark touching the right angle mark, extend the sleeve
    to 3/4" length and make 5" wide.

11. Front arm divided by 2 - 1/2" = 5". Make 3/4" line 5".

12. Before connecting underarm line, measure armhole body to determine if
    line is the same length. Make the line longer at the star mark.

Raglan Sleeve

Back Body

1. Extend 1/2" to shoulder.

2. Draw dotted line at underarm.

3. Mark up 3/8" and square.

4. On the squared line go up 1-1/4" and mark.

5. New neck line down 1/2" and connect to underarm. Find center and mark 1/4" out (toward shoulder) and curve.

6. Measure down 1/2" at underarm curve.

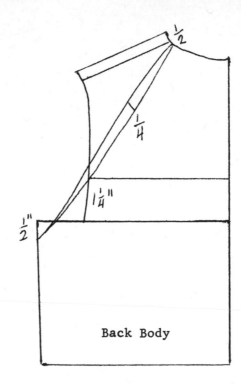

Back Body

Back Sleeve

1. Make diagram like the above.

2. Finish the sleeve like the front, including the 1/2" on shoulder.

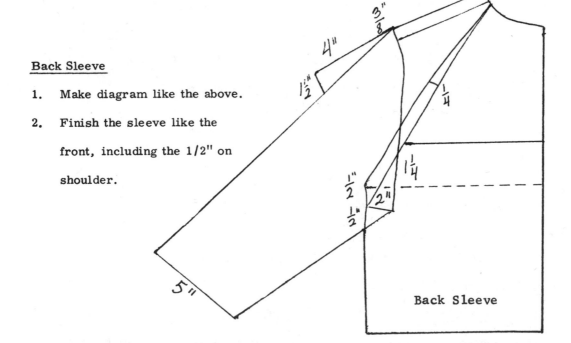

Back Sleeve

22

New Fabrics

Wet Look or Vinyl Trimmed Dress

This vinyl yoke stretch knit dress introduces some of the new fabrics. The "wet look" yoke follows the yoke technique described in Chapter 8. Since this fabric cannot be ironed, glue the seam allowance to itself and then to the dress using buttonhole twist. The vinyl collar and tab have also been top-stitched. Covered buttons accent the yoke as well as the tab which is sewn from the neck edge to the bottom edge of the yoke. No darts are drawn in the dress front. Use the basic short sleeve described on page 45. The back has the same vinyl yoke as the front, waistline darts and a zipper closing.

The snakeskin pattern on the vinyl fabric can be used for collars, tab fronts, pockets, sleeve bands, belts and even as a band around the bottom of a too short dress. It is easy to sew, but remember to glue instead of iron.

Sewing with Leather

Leather can also be easily made into a fashionable outfit. Try making a skirt, vest and purse from the new bright-colored leathers.

The skirt is made like the A-line skirt in this book. Do not make a waist band. The seams cannot be ironed, but open them and glue them flat to the skirt using rubber cement. Pound the seams on the right side with a wooden mallet so the seam will lie flat. Glue the hem to the skirt. Put a zipper in the skirt back by gluing back the seam allowance. Then tape the zipper to the leather with long strips of scotch tape so the zipper won't slip when sewing. Sew the zipper in the skirt, remove the tape. Make a lining like the skirt, sew to the top of the skirt right sides to right sides. Turn lining to the inside and stitch in the dart line down 1/2". Make a hem in the lining.

The vest is drawn as a blouse with a round neck. Cut down the front and curve at the desired position on the body.

The shoulder purse is drawn in two pieces and a gusset. Half of the outside bag section folds over and is cut in 1/2" strips to resemble fringe. The second section, or lower half of the bag, is sewn to the gusset on one side, then the second piece of the bag is sewn to the gusset. The handle is attached using pocketbook fasteners that can be purchased in the leather stores. Make this bag any desired size. My total bag, before folding measures 22" long. The upper section measures 9" wide and the lower section measures 10" wide. The second section measures 9" long and 10" wide. Draw a curve around the edges. The gusset measures 14" long and 2-1/2" inches at the top, tapering to 3-1/2" at the bottom. Cut the fringe 6-1/2" from outside edge toward the bag in strips 1/2" wide.

Stretch Fabrics

Use any of the designs in this book for stretch fabrics. Stretch knit fabrics are care-easy sew fabrics. When sewing on these fabrics be sure to use a ballpoint needle, and nine stitches to the inch. Wash the fabric and dry it before cutting.

Try making stretch slacks with elastic in the top using the slacks techniques in this book -- omitting the darts. Sew elastic to the top edge of the slacks after sewing the elastic together. Make the elastic 1" smaller than waistline measurement and lap 1/2". After sewing the elastic to the top edge, turn to the wrong side and sew the top edge to the slacks. To flare the leg, add equal amounts to both sides of the leg at the point on the leg where you want the flare. The flare can start at mid calf or lower as desired.

Appendix 1

Simplified Clothing Construction

By revealing the patternless dressmaking techniques discovered in the Orient centuries ago this practical book tells how to design and sew clothes without pre-cut patterns, expensive dress forms or other costly sewing aids. All you do is find a picture of the outfit you want to make and the instructions on how to make each element, from the sleeves to the skirt or pants, is here in this book. The clothes will be superior in fit, quality and durability, and more a reflection of your own style than anything you could buy.

EQUIPMENT

To make home sewing easy and accurate, you need the proper equipment and supplies. Check the items listed below for aids that will be useful to you.

Cutting and Sewing Aids

Cutting shears.—At least 8 inches long, with blades that cut precisely to the point.

Scissors.—Small ones, about 5 inches long for such work as cutting threads.

Pins.—Silk dressmaker pins, size 16. This size is suitable for working on most fabrics.

Tape measure.—Get one that will not stretch, either of fabric or a rollup metal.

Colored-chalk pencils.—For easy marking of pattern perforations; the marks can be brushed off quickly when no longer needed.

Needles for hand sewing.—Size 7 or 8 needles are strong enough for sewing heavy fabrics such as work cottons. A finer needle, size 9 or 10, is easier to use on fine wools, silks, cottons, and other lightweight fabrics. Crewel needles, those with large eyes, are easy to thread. There are also needles with "threaders" attached; they are good for basting.

Thimble.—Get a thimble that fits snugly so it will not drop off the finger while sewing, but not so tight as to be uncomfortable. When buying a thimble, try it on for a perfect fit.

Colored thread.—Contrasting basing thread is easy to follow when stitching.

Ruler, 6-inch transparent.—Get a ruler with ⅛-inch markings on both sides and ends. It can be used as a guide when basting or marking seam widths and corners.

Cloth guide.—A machine attachment to guide to the edge of the fabric while stitching. Aids in making the stitching even.

Seam-width marker.—A small gummed marker to be fastened on to the machine throat plate. Saves time when the cloth guide needs adjusting. Throat plates with permanent indications of stitching width are now available on many machines.

Bias cutting guide.—A small attachment to be slipped on a scissor blade to aid in cutting bias strips of fabric evenly.

Pencil sharpener.—Get a small, inexpensive one for keeping sharp points on pencils to be used for marking notches and perforations.

Hem marker.—Get an accurate one for marking skirt lengths. Hem markers requiring a second person to pin the length are more accurate than those that are self-operating.

Stiletto.—A sharp instrument for punching eyelets and removing bastings.

Ironing Aids

Careful pressing often saves basting and is a help in producing attractive, well-made garments. The following equipment is needed for pressing:

Iron.—Preferably an automatic one, with a temperature indicator which prevents damage to heat-sensitive fabrics.

Ironing board.—Have a well-padded ironing board that can be lowered to sitting height. It is convenient for small pressing jobs and can serve also as a sewing table between pressings.

Press cloths.—These cloths are needed for pressing fabrics likely to be damaged by direct contact with the iron. There are many good ones specially treated to make pressing effective—heavy cotton ones for use on wools, non-woven cloths for most materials, and those made of organdie with see-through qualities.

Sponge.—A cellulose sponge for dampening fabrics or press cloths; it spreads the moisture evenly and is more serviceable than natural sponges.

Water container.—A convenience at the ironing board. Use the lid to rest the sponge on between usings.

Machine-Attachment Aids

Some sewing processes can be done quickly and satisfactorily by machine, particularly on work and school clothes. Buttonholes, hems, seam finishing can be done on a swing-needle machine, or by means of the following special machine attachments:

Buttonholer.—A useful attachment for making buttonholes on men's shirts, on housedresses, and on school clothes.

Edge-stitcher.—For keeping outside stitching very close to the edge.

Gathering foot.—For gathering long lengths of fabric.

Narrow hemmer.—For making tiny hems on ruffles.

Overcaster.—For finishing seam edges on fabrics that fray badly.

Ruffler.—For gathering such things as skirts into small, flat pleats.

Zigzagger.—For finishing seam edges of such fabrics as rayons, linens, and some wools that will fray badly.

MATERIALS

When time is limited and there is much sewing to do, look for materials that are easy to handle.

- Firm, closely woven fabrics are easy to cut out, can often be finger pressed, and so save frequent trips to the ironing board. Because such fabrics don't fray, they need little seam finishing. Ginghams, percales, and dressweight chambrays are examples of materials that can usually be made up quickly.

- Plain colors, allover prints, or small woven checks or stripes can be cut out and put together more quickly than larger plaids or stripes that must be matched to look well. It takes time and painstaking care to match plaids or stripes in cutting and putting together a garment.

- Less material is needed for prints with no up and down than for directional prints, and less time is required to lay out the pattern. Less material is also needed for reversible fabrics that are the same on both sides than for fabrics with a right and a wrong side.

Some materials require careful sewing and skillful handling and take more time to make up well.

- Slippery fabrics, such as silk or synthetic sheers, are hard to cut out because they twist and slip; they also are hard to sew accurately.
- Loosely woven fabrics—voiles, silk or synthetic sheers, linens and rayons with a linen look, and tweeds—need a special seam finish to prevent fraying, so take extra time.
- Some materials are hard to sew. Very closely woven ones, such as balloon cloth, some of those treated with special finishes, and others made of some of the new manmade fibers, need special thread and machine adjustments to prevent puckered stitching. Pile fabrics, too—velvet, velveteen, and corduroy—need careful basting to keep the material from slipping as it is being stitched. All these materials are also hard to press.

Straightening the material before the pattern pieces are laid on it assures that the clothes will hang as well after washing or cleaning as they did before. Fabrics are always woven so the lengthwise yarns are at right angles to the crosswise ones, but they are often distorted in finishing so they look crooked.

When material needs to be straightened, first see that each end of the fabric is cut along a crosswise yarn. Many cottons, such as percale, chambray, and gingham, and some silk crepes, taffetas, and wool flannels can usually be straightened at the ends by tearing them crosswise. Other materials, such as voile, linen, spun rayon, sateens, and many novelty weaves, do not tear satisfactorily, so the ends should be straightened by pulling out one or two crosswise yarns and cutting along the open spaces. Materials with heavy crosswise yarns that are easy to follow can be cut along one of these yarns. If the yarns at each end seem to run downhill instead of straight across, the material needs to be straightened.

Most fabrics can be straightened by stretching the material on the bias between the low corner at one end and the opposite selvage, and then pulling crosswise from selvage to selvage. Cottons with glazed or other special finishes may have to be folded lengthwise, pinned across the ends and along the selvages, and then steam pressed, pulling the yarns into position as you press. Some of these materials may need to be wet thoroughly, then pulled into shape and ironed. Wools, if they are very crooked, may need to be steam pressed. Press out the lengthwise fold after the fabric is straightened.

PATTERNS*

Select a pattern carefully. A pattern that is the right size can save alteration and fitting time. Before a pattern is bought, it is important to check certain body measurements—chest, bust or breast, waist, hip, arm length, and back length. These measurements can be compared with those in the charts in the pattern books as a guide to classification and size of the pattern to buy. For irregular figures, patterns should be altered before the garment is cut out.

For beginners or those who have much sewing to do, it is a good idea to use patterns with style features that can be made well in a fairly short time and that need a minimum of fitting. Some style features to consider are the following:

Sleeves.—Kimono (fig. 1), raglan (fig. 2), or shirt-type sleeves are easier to fit and make than set-in (fig. 3) or epaulet (fig. 4) styles. Underarm gussets (fig. 5) make close-fitting kimono sleeves more comfortable, but since the corners are weak, they require careful reinforcement and therefore take more time and skill to make than the ordinary kimono sleeve.

*These guidelines are often helpful to the beginner. Patterns are not necessary after learning the techniques in this book.

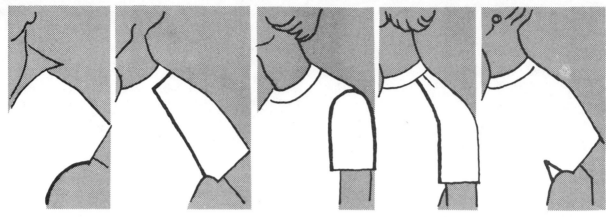

FIGURE 1 FIGURE 2 FIGURE 3 FIGURE 4 FIGURE 5

Collars.—Collars with square corners (fig. 6) or with shallow curves (fig. 7) are easier to make well than those with sharp points (fig. 8) or deep curves (fig. 9) which require careful stitching, trimming, and clipping so that when turned they will be smooth with no bumpy edges or corners.

Neck finishes.—V-necklines (fig. 10) or collars sewed to V-necks are likely to stretch as they are being sewed, and may need extra stitching and careful handling to prevent stretching. Collars cut in one with the front of the blouse are not likely to stretch at the neck.

Shoulder fitting.—Shoulder tucks (fig. 11) are usually simple to make and easier to adjust than shoulder darts (fig. 12) when the shoulders need to be widened or narrowed.

Yokes.—Straight corstruction lines in some yokes and necklines require less time to sew and are likely to look better when finished than bias or curved lines (fig. 13), which must be stitched very carefully to avoid stretching and sometimes must be sewed over paper.

Pockets.—Patch pockets, or those cut in with (fig. 14) or sewed to a seam, are quicker and easier to make and are usually more durable than bound or slit pockets (fig. 15), which require careful pressing, stitching, and clipping.

Skirts.—Gathered skirts (fig. 16), those with six or more gores, and those with unpressed pleats are easier to fit than skirts with pressed pleats, or those with two, three, or four gores.

CUTTING

For ease in cutting a garment, lay out the material, right sides together, so the marking can be done on the wrong side. Then place the pattern pieces accurately on the material according to the pattern layout suggested for the size and width of the fabric. Make sure the straight-of-goods marks are an even distance from the selvage, so each garment section will be cut exactly with the grain of the goods.

Accurate cutting saves time. Smooth seam edges are easier to sew evenly and to hold

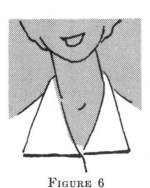

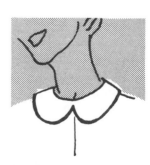

FIGURE 6 FIGURE 7 FIGURE 8 FIGURE 9

FIGURE 10

FIGURE 11

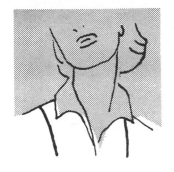

FIGURE 12

FIGURE 13

against the cloth stitching guide than those that are uneven and jagged.

Some women like to save time by cutting several garments at once. For this purpose the layers of fabric must be laid out perfectly straight and smooth, with the edges pinned carefully together to keep the material from slipping. Care must be taken that all the necessary pieces are provided for and cut out; when the fabric is laid out in single layers, it is easy to forget the second sleeve or collar. Extra time will be needed for sections that must be laid on a lengthwise fold of the material, and for accurately marking the pattern perforations.

More than six layers of lightweight material, such as gingham, chambray, or percale, are extremely hard to pin and cut at one time with home equipment. Six layers mean that three garments from the double fabric, or six garments from opened-out fabric can be cut, but this cutting requires a pair of sturdy, bent-handle shears and a strong hand. Smaller scissors are not heavy enough. When several garments are to be cut out at once, patterns with simple, straight lines are easier to manage.

MARKING

Time can be saved in putting the garment together if all the necessary pattern perforations, such as those for darts, pleats, plackets, and buttonholes, are marked before the tissue pattern is unpinned. However, all the stitching lines may not need to be marked. For example, seam allowances need not be marked if the seam width allowed in the pattern is carefully followed. Straight darts can be marked at the wide section and at the point; then a guideline for stitching can be drawn between these two points at the left of the fold.

Construction lines may be marked in several ways:

Colored-chalk pencil and colored-carbon paper.—These materials afford an easy way of marking most firmly woven materials since two garment pieces can be marked at once. Place

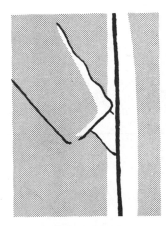

FIGURE 14

FIGURE 15

FIGURE 16

the carbon under the garment section and mark lightly on the top section with the pencil sharpened to a fine point, so the marks won't show when the garment is finished. Be sure to mark only on the wrong side of the fabric. A small ruler and the pencil and carbon paper may be used to draw short stitching lines.

Tracing wheel and colored-carbon paper.— A tracing wheel is used the same way as the colored pencil and the carbon paper, but the tracing wheel is harder to guide than a pencil and leaves more marks that are hard to remove.

Tailor's tacks.—Tailor's tacks may be used for transferring pattern markings to loosely woven materials and some allover prints where chalk or tracing-wheel marks might not show readily. Make them of contrasting embroidery cotton which has little tendency to pull out of the material. Remove the threads before machine stitching, as they are hard to get out once they are caught in with the stitching.

Pins.—Darts, tucks, and pleats can be marked with clean pins that won't leave dark marks when they are removed. Pin through both layers in the center of the pattern marking; then lift the material carefully and put a pin through the bottom layer in the hole made by the first pin. Anchor each pin firmly so it won't drop out. Pins have an advantage over pencil or tracing marks as the pins can be seen on both the right and the wrong sides.

Snips.—In the seam edges, notches or dart ends may be marked by making a very short straight cut or snip in the center of each notch or in line with perforations. Snips should be used sparingly, as they may interfere with alterations.

BASTING

For best results some type of basting is usually needed to hold two pieces of a garment together for fitting or stitching.

Pin-basting.—If no fitting will be needed, straight edges in firm materials may be held adequately with pins put in at right angles to the edge, but enough pins must be used to keep the material flat and the seam edges together. This method is called pin-basting. Put the pins in so they can be taken out with the free hand during stitching and thus avoid sewing over the pins and breaking or blunting the machine needle. Another way of pin-basting firm materials is to place the pins about 1 inch from the edge and parallel to it. This saves stitching time and also eliminates the danger of breaking or blunting the needle. Pin-basting should not be used on slippery materials such as synthetic sheers or on pile fabrics—the edges will not stay together unless they are held more securely.

Machine-basting.—This basting, made with long machine stitches about 6 or 8 to the inch, is a quick way of getting a garment ready for fitting, and the basting lines can be made straight. Such basting is harder to take out than hand-basting, and it cannot be pulled out quickly while the garment is being fitted, which is sometimes necessary.

Hand-basting is particularly helpful when sewing curved edges as on collars, or putting in sleeves, or when considerable fitting needs to be done.

Slip-basting—catching a folded edge to a flat section with slip stitches—is necessary when basting needs to be done from the right side as when matching uneven plaids or doing intricate seaming.

A combination of pin and thread-basting may be the most satisfactory method for most sewing. Time can often be saved by pinning together such edges as skirt seams, shoulder and underarm seams, and sleeve seams. However, when setting in sleeves or attaching a collar to a neck, basting helps to make the stitching quick, easy, and more accurate.

To thread-baste, use a contrasting thread and baste slightly outside the stitching line so the basting will not get caught in with the stitching. Cut off basting knots before stitching to keep from sewing them in with the stitching.

MACHINE SEWING

A cloth or seam guide (fig. 17) is a most useful machine attachment for sewing seams. Fasten it the width of the seam allowance from the needle point; then hold the seam edges steadily against it during the stitching. If the seam edges are even, the stitching line will be even. This guide works equally well for edge stitching.

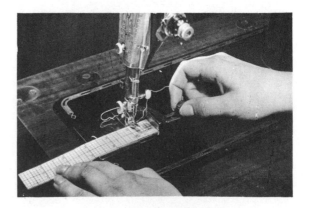

FIGURE 17

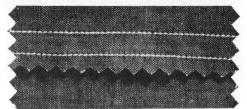

FIGURE 18

FIGURE 19

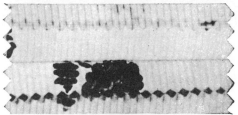

FIGURE 20

FIGURE 21

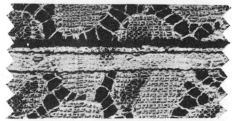

FIGURE 22

FIGURE 23

Stitches of an ordinary length, between 12 and 16 to the inch, are good for most home sewing. When stitching around points or into corners where the material will be cut close to the stitching, shorten the stitch to around 20 and 25 to the inch. Use reverse stitching on inside seams where it is essential that the stitching does not open. Reverse stitches should not be used on outside stitching where appearance is important, or at the ends of darts, as reverse stitches rarely fit exactly into stitches made with the forward motion and make the stitching bulky. Reverse stitching is particularly useful on school or utility clothes.

Choose a seam finish suited to the material and the garment. Plain seams may be adequate on fabrics that are firm and do not fray easily. Materials that fray, or are bulky, need special seam finishing for durability and professional appearance.

Double-stitched and pinked seam (fig. 18).— For use on cotton wash clothes made of firmly woven fabrics, such as gingham, percale, and chambray. These seams are durable, firm, and easy to make; they also are easy to iron as they iron straight and smooth from the right side, and the double stitching keeps them from stretching.

Closed and zigzagged seam (fig. 19).—For use on sleazy, loosely woven, or easily frayed fabrics that need special seam finishing. Machine-zigzagging or overcasting usually keeps such materials from fraying. This seam is also easy to iron from the right side.

Opened and pinked seam (fig. 20).—For use on thick or heavy fabrics, such as embossed or sculptured cottons, and some silks, rayons, and wools that do not fray.

Opened, stitched, and pinked seam (fig. 21).— For use on wool jersey or on bias seams; the extra rows of stitching help prevent stretching and also keep jersey seams from rolling.

Double-stitched and trimmed seam (fig. 22).— For use on laces and eyelet embroideries that require a flat, narrow, inconspicuous, yet durable seam.

Opened and overcast seam (fig. 23).—For use on heavier fabrics that may fray, such as linen, cotton crash, linen-weave silks and rayons, and denim. The edges may be overcast by hand or zigzagged on a swing-needle machine or with a special attachment.

FIGURE 24

FIGURE 25

FIGURE 26

FIGURE 27

FIGURE 28

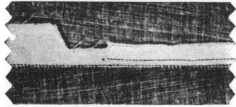

FIGURE 29

French seam (fig. 24).—For use on sheer cottons, silks, and synthetics, such as voiles and sheer fabrics, that are likely to fray badly.

Self-stitched seam (fig. 25).—For use on fabrics that fray too much to be overcast. This seam is also used on unlined jackets or coats of cottons, rayons, and some lightweight wools.

Zigzagged seam (fig. 26).—For use on lingerie materials. It is stitched on the wrong side, pressed to one side, then zigzagged from the right side over the seam line. It is an elastic seam so is often used on slips. It is hard to wash clean, especially if dark clothes rub against a light-colored seam.

Flat-fell seam (fig. 27).—For use on men's and boys' shirts and work clothes. This seam with no raw edges is durable, but has a tendency to pucker with laundering and is hard to iron. It takes longer to make than many other seams.

Mock flat-fell seam (fig. 28).—For use on men's and boys' shirts and work clothes when a flat-fell seam is too heavy.. It resembles a flat-fell seam in outside appearance, but is less bulky and easier to make. On the wrong side it has one raw edge which can be pinked or zigzagged if the fabric frays.

Bound seam (fig. 29).—For use on fabrics that fray badly. Net footing when used to bind seams on colored sheers, such as voile, makes the seams look less heavy than French seams. Rayon binding makes a neat seam finish for unlined jackets and coats of wool; on fabrics of manmade fibers, however, binding leaves an imprint on the right side.

ORGANIZING HOME SEWING

Time can be saved by organizing home sewing—planning how much stitching can be done at one time without interfering with the next steps—then how much trimming, turning, basting, and pressing are necessary before the next trip to the machine. Although planning is particularly easy when a garment can be made up without any fitting, it also helps to reduce the number of fittings.

A sport shirt is used here to illustrate how planned construction can save time. The same procedure can be followed, whether one shirt or several are to be made (fig. 30).

Pin:
1. Back pleats.
2. Yoke and yoke facing to back.
3. Shoulders of yoke facing to shirt fronts.
4. Interfacing to undercollar.

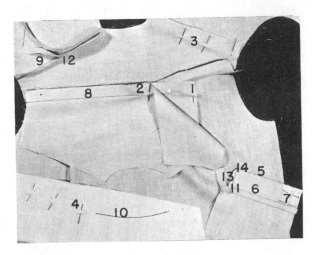

FIGURE 30

Fold:
   5. Pocket hem to right side.
   6. Pocket hem up about ¼ inch. Finger-press.

Pin:
   7. Pocket hem edges.

Stitch:
   8. Yoke and yoke facing to back.
   9. Shoulders of yoke facing to shirt fronts.
  10. Interfacing to undercollar along crease marks.
  11. Pocket hem edges a seam's width and the depth of the hem.

Trim:
  12. Shoulder seams.
  13. Pocket hem edges.

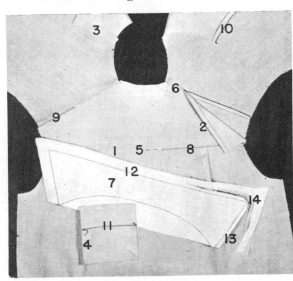

FIGURE 31

Clip:
  14. Corners of pocket seams.
Press as much as possible, baste where necessary, then continue the stitching.
  Press (fig. 31):
   1. Yoke and yoke facing toward neck.
   2. Turn under and press shoulder seams of yoke.
   3. Turn under and press shoulder and front edges of facings.
   4. Turn pocket hem right side out; turn under sides and bottom of pocket; press.
Pin, baste, if necessary:
   5. Back yokes together.
   6. Shoulder seams of yoke over seam of yoke facing, covering the machine-stitching.
   7. Top collar to undercollar and interfacing.
Stitch:
   8. Back yokes about ⅛ inch above seam line.
   9. Shoulder seams of yoke.
  10. Shoulders and front edges of facings.
  11. Pocket hem.
  12. Top collar to undercollar and interfacing.
Trim:
  13. Seam edges of collar to ¼ inch.
Clip:
  14. Collar corners, almost to stitching.

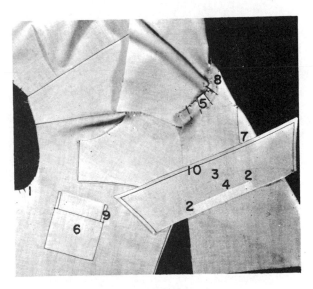

FIGURE 32

Clip (fig. 32):
   1. Armhole edges at underarm area, cutting about ⅜ inch deep.
   2. Top collar at shoulder points, cutting in a seam's depth.
Turn:
   3. Collar right side out.
   4. Seam allowance of top collar under between shoulder points.

Pin, baste, if necessary:

   5. Sleeve to armhole, stretching shirt armhole at underarm to fit sleeve.
   6. Pocket to shirt front.
   7 Collar edges, with seam line on the edge; work the corners out to a point; finger press or press.

Stitch:

   8. Sleeve to armhole.
   9. Pocket to shirt front.
  10. Around collar the desired width from the edge.

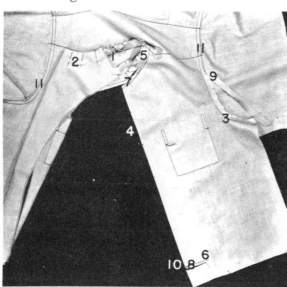

FIGURE 33

Pin (fig. 33):

   1. Collar to neckline.
   2. Front facings back over neck.

Press:

   3. Armhole seams toward sleeve.
   4. Front facing edges.

Stitch:

   5. Collar to neck and facing.
   6. Bottom of front facings, even with the hemline.

Trim:

   7. Neck seam edge to $\frac{1}{8}$ or $\frac{3}{16}$ inch.
   8. Seam at bottom of front facing to $\frac{1}{8}$ inch.
   9. Armhole seam allowance of sleeve to $\frac{3}{16}$ inch.

Clip:

  10. Corner at front edges.

Stitch:

  11. Finish seams as flat fell, mock flat fell, or leave plain and pink or zigzag, if necessary, to prevent fraying.

Stitch (fig. 34):

   1. Underarm and sleeve seams.

Turn and press; baste, if necessary:

   2. Front facings back to wrong side.
   3. Seams.
   4. Vent hems, if vents are desired.
   5. Shirt hem.
   6. Sleeve hems.
   7. Neck edge of collar to back of neck.

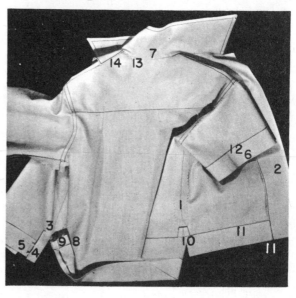

FIGURE 34

Stitch:

   8. At vent, turn hem to right side, stitch vent through hem on the side seam line.

Trim:

   9. Vent seam edge to $\frac{1}{4}$ inch.

Turn and press:

  10. Vent and hem to wrong side, creasing on stitching line.

Stitch:

  11. Shirt hem and around vents beginning at bottom of front facing.
  12. Sleeve hem.
  13. Back neck edge of collar to neck of shirt.
  14. Shoulder edges of front facings to shoulder seams.

NOTE.—13 and 14 may be stitched by hand or by machine.

Dresses, blouses, and other garments can be made as efficiently as shirts, provided they do not require fitting. Stitch all darts or tucks; attach the cloth or seam guide and sew all the seams; stitch the collars and cuffs; then lengthen the stitch and do all the gathering necessary while the cloth guide is in place. This gathering may include sleeve caps, waistline edges of skirt or blouse, or elbow ease, depending on the style. After as much of the stitching has been done as possible, trim seam allowances where needed, snip corners, pink or edge-finish the seams, turn collars and cuffs right side out, and press so every edge will be ready for the next stitching.

SIMPLIFYING CONSTRUCTION

Much of the detailed work of sewing—so important to the good appearance of a finished garment—can be simplified without either durability or good workmanship being sacrificed. In fact, appearance is often improved by the flat construction characteristic of the simplified procedures presented in the following pages. To simplify sewing does not necessarily mean the elimination of basting, when basting is necessary to help achieve the desired results; it may also mean the inclusion of some extra steps which may take a little extra time, but will make the construction process easier to do. For example, taking time to trim the seam allowance of a curved collar to ⅛ or ³⁄₁₆ inch saves time in turning the collar, and results in a more even collar edge than would be possible if the seam edge were not trimmed.

Making Collars

Round collars.—Round collars are used on many types of garments, but the method of making them is the same. The curve at each end of the collar must be identical; to make it so, draw a stitching line around each curve with a cup, saucer, or other round object of the right size being used as the pattern; or, make a paper pattern. To make the collar—

1. Seam the top and the undercollars together, right sides inside (fig. 35). If the material is soft and likely to stretch, make a whole

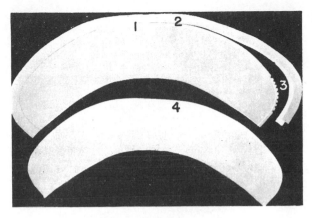

FIGURE 36

paper pattern and sew through it; or use a thin interfacing of preshrunk fabric.

2. Trim the seam allowance to ³⁄₁₆ or ⅛ inch (fig. 36); bevel the edges of thick materials; that is, trim one edge about ¹⁄₁₆ inch narrower than the other.

3. Clip out small wedges of the seam around the curves to avoid lumpiness and so make a smooth flat edge when turned.

4. Turn the collar right side out; crease on the seam line; baste to keep it in place until the collar is stitched to the garment; press. On thick materials, ease the seam line slightly to the under side to keep it from rolling to the right side and showing.

Shirt collars.—Shirt collars are used on sport shirts, blouses, dresses, and on some jackets and coats. Lighter weight garments, such as dresses and blouses, are made the same way, but usually the stitching in Step 1, figure 37, is omitted.

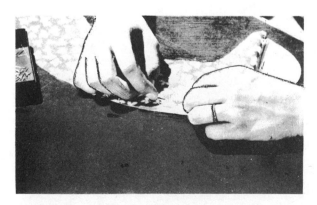

FIGURE 35

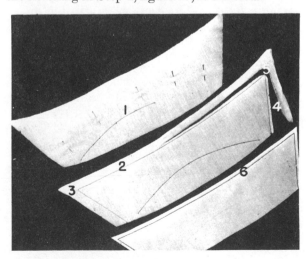

FIGURE 37

1. Pin the interfacing to the undercollar; stitch on the perforations marking the roll line.

2. Pin the top collar to the undercollar, interfacing outside. Draw a straight stitching line on each end of the collar; a bias edge such as this is hard to stitch exactly straight, even with a seam guide, and a guideline helps. Adjust the stitches to about 20 to the inch and stitch around the collar edges a seam's width from the edge.

3. Take one stitch across the corner, instead of pivoting the ends. This stitch allows room for the seam edges when the collar is turned right side out. If the material is thick or bulky, about three stitches around the corner may be needed.

4. Trim the seam allowance to about ⅛ inch on firm materials, 3/16 inch on fabrics that are likely to fray.

5. Clip off the corners almost to the stitching, so they will be sharp and flat when turned.

6. Turn the collar right side out, with the seam on the edge; work the corners out carefully to a point; a blunt darning needle is good for this. Baste, if necessary; press. Stitch evenly around the outside edge of the collar the desired width from the edge. This stitching gives a sharp edge and makes ironing easy but is often omitted on dresses, blouses, and outerwear.

Attaching Collars

Collars sewed on with a shaped facing.—The following method is a quick and easy one for attaching collars to school and utility clothes. However, it is not generally used on better garments, as the neckline is rather bulky and therefore does not set so well to the neck as when a bias facing is used. Also, it does not press or iron so well (fig. 38).

1. Seam the front and the back facings together at the shoulder. Clip the seam ends diagonally to the stitching so the neck and outer edges will be less bulky when finished.

2. Turn the outer edge of the facing under and machine-stitch; or pink or zigzag the edge, depending on the firmness of the material.

3. Clip the neck edge of the blouse and the facing about ¼ inch deep and ¼ inch apart; this makes it easier to fit the neck edges together.

4. Pin the collar to the neck of the blouse.

5. Turn and pin the front facings back over the collar.

6. Pin the shaped facing to the collar and the neckline, matching the shoulder seams.

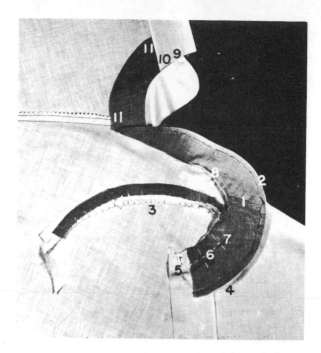

FIGURE 38

7. Baste with rather small stitches to hold the collar in place and to make a guideline for stitching; machine-stitch.

8. Trim the seam allowance to ¼ inch or less.

9. Turn the collar to the outside and facing to the inside; press.

10. To keep the facing from rolling up, stitch it around the neck edge close to the collar, sewing only the facing and the neck seam.

11. Tack the neck facing to the shoulder seams, the center front facings, and the back darts, to keep it in place during wear and cleaning.

Collars sewed on with a bias facing.—Most collars set to the neck better if they are sewed on with a bias facing, but the facing must be smooth, flat and narrow—about ¼ inch wide or less, depending on the material. On lightweight wash fabrics use a facing of self-material, or a commercial bias binding; on wool garments use matching silk or rayon. On medium weight or heavier materials, such as gingham, cotton, crash, linen, and some wools, use a single facing.

On thin fabrics, such as voile or batiste, use a double facing, which is easy to put on. Cut it twice the seam allowance width, plus the desired width of the finished facing. A double facing is shown in figure 39.

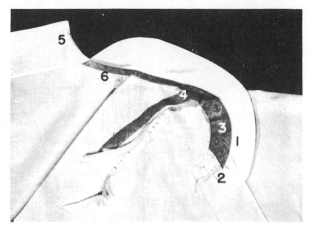

FIGURE 39

1. Pin the collar to the neckline, clipping the curved neck edges as needed.

2. Turn the front facing in place back over the collar and pin.

3. Steam-press and curve the bias to almost the same shape as the curved neck edge (see Binding, page 13); then pin the shaped bias strip to the collar and the neck edge. Baste with stitches short enough to hold a good curved line. Machine-stitch.

4. Trim the neck seam allowance to about 3/16 inch or less; clip where necessary to make it lie flat.

5. Turn the facing to the inside of the garment. Press. Press the bias facing flat against the blouse.

6. Sew the bias facing edge to the blouse, catching in the edge of the front facing. Machine-stitching may be used on school, play, or utility clothes; use hand sewing on better garments.

Convertible collar—sport-shirt method.— This method is a quick one for attaching a straight or shaped collar to sport shirts or school or work clothes. It is not suited to better garments where a flat neck join is desirable (fig. 40).

FIGURE 40

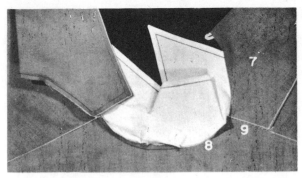

FIGURE 41

1. Clip the top collar a seam's depth at the shoulder points. Turn under this seam allowance across the back between the shoulder points.

2. Pin the collar to the neckline; snip the curved neck edges where needed.

3. Pin or stitch a fabric loop to the left front neck, if for a boy's or man's shirt.

4. Turn and pin the front facings back over the collar, the neck edges matching. Baste, if needed.

5. Machine-stitch the neck seam, being careful not to catch the turned-up edge of the top collar.

6. Trim the seam allowance to about 1/4 inch.

7. Turn the facings to the wrong side (fig. 41).

8. Pin or baste the loose edge of the top collar over the machine-stitching. Machine-stitch over the neck seam or hem by hand.

9. Sew the facings to the shoulder seam, by hand or machine.

Convertible collar—dressmaker method.— This method gives a smooth flat front joining of the collar with the facing, and is suitable to use on better clothes and some tailored garments such as coats and suits. The collar pieces are attached to the facing and neck edges and then the collar is completed (fig. 42).

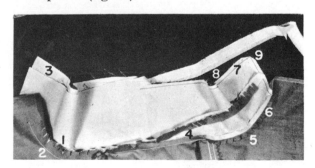

FIGURE 42

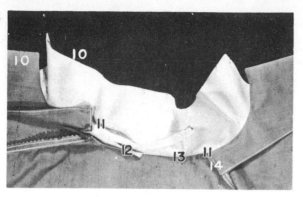

FIGURE 43

1. Clip the curved neck edges to within ¼ inch of the seam line so it can be fitted to a straight collar.

2. Pin, baste, and stitch the undercollar to the neck of the blouse.

3. Pin, baste, and stitch the top collar to the two front facings.

4. Trim the neck seam allowances to ¼ inch.

5. Clip the tight curved edges.

6. Press the seams open.

7. Pin, baste, and stitch the top collar and the facings to the undercollar and the blouse fronts, right sides together.

8. Trim the seam allowances to ⅛ or ¼ inch.

9. Clip the corners almost to the stitching, so they will be sharp and flat when turned.

10. Turn the collar and the facings right side out, with the seam right on the edge on lightweight fabrics; on wools or heavier materials, roll the seam line slightly to the underside. Baste (fig. 43).

11. Clip the top collar at the shoulder points to the seam line.

12. Trim the collar seam allowance across the back of the neck to ¼ inch. Turn under to the seam line.

13. Sew the collar to the back neck seam by hand.

14. Tack the shoulder edges of the front facings to the shoulder seams by hand.

Finishing Edges

Binding.—A strong, easy-to-make neck or sleeve finish (fig. 44).

1. Dampen and press a single- or a double-bias binding so it has almost the same curve as the neck. When a single binding is used, leave the outer edge folded. Preshaped binding fits smoothly to a curved edge and insures a better finish than when the binding is eased on.

2. Baste and stitch to neck. If a commercial binding is used, lay the inside fold line against

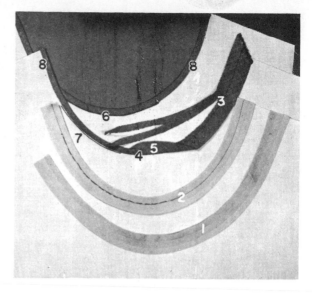

FIGURE 44

the seam line, or trim the neck seam to the same width.

3. If a double binding is used, stitch to the neck, then trim the seam allowance to ⅛ or 3/16 inch.

4. Press the seams and binding toward the neck.

5. Fold the binding smoothly over the seam edges, working from the right side to insure an even width.

6. If the binding is to be sewed down by machine, fold it so the edge comes about 1/16 inch past the seam line. Baste; press.

7. Machine-stitch from the right side, very close to the seam line.

8. If the binding is to be sewed down by hand, make the folded edge come just inside the seam line. Baste, press. Then sew by hand to the first row of stitching.

Facing.—A smooth, flat finish for collarless necks, sleeves without cuffs, or sleeveless garments; also for front openings and other edges. If the pattern does not include facings, they can be cut according to the pattern edge to be faced (fig. 45)

1. Stitch any seams necessary in the facing, as at the shoulders, and press open. Be sure before stitching that the facing fits the garment edge exactly.

2. Stitch the facing to the garment.

3. Trim the seam allowance to ¼ inch. Clip any corners almost to the stitching.

4. Press the seam edge and the facing away from the garment.

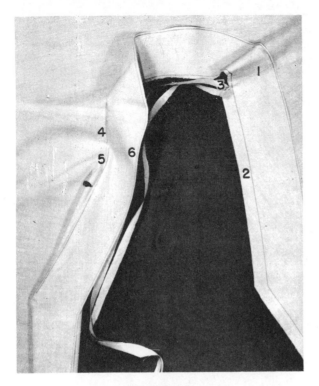

FIGURE 45

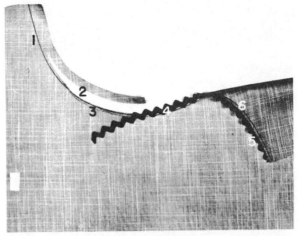

FIGURE 46

5. Stitch the seam edges and the facing together close to the neck seam line, taking care not to stitch through the garment. This stitching helps keep the faced edge flat and the seam line slightly underneath.

6. Finish the inside edge of the facing, either with pinking, or with zigzagging, or by turning and stitching, according to the firmness of the material. Tack the facing firmly to the darts and the seams; if it needs to be fastened to the body of the garment, use tiny, loose stitches spaced an inch or so apart so they will not show or pucker on the right side.

Rickrack.—An edge finish that is strong, attractive, and practical for school and utility clothes made of materials that do not fray badly. Shown here as a finish for a neckline (fig. 46).

1. Machine-stitch a fold line slightly less than a seam's width from the edge to be finished.

2. Trim the seam allowance to $\frac{1}{8}$ inch.

3. Turn the seam edge to the wrong side, folding just past the stitching line; press.

4. Pin and baste the rickrack over the fold so that only the points show on the right side.

5. On the right side, machine-stitch close to the fold.

6. Stitch again on the right side, the width of the presser foot beyond the first stitching. This second row of stitching holds the inside points of the rickrack and the raw edges flat.

Finishing Hems

Suit the hem finish to the material and the type of garment. However, in all dress, skirt, or coat hems, the first step is to mark the length an even distance from the floor. To measure, hold the ruler straight or use a measuring device that stands upright (fig. 75). Turn up the hem on these marks; pin, baste, and press. Then trim the material so the hem is an even width from the fold (fig. 76).

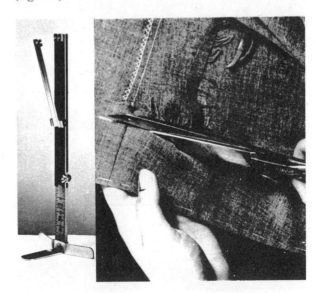

FIGURE 75   FIGURE 76

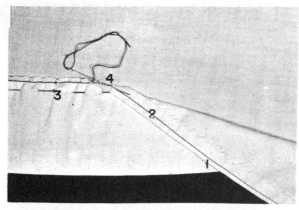

FIGURE 77

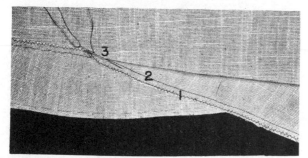

FIGURE 78

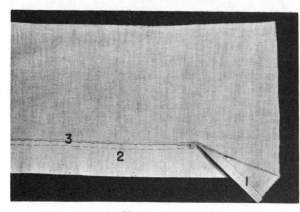

FIGURE 79

FIGURE 80

Turned and slip-stitched hems.—For use on light- and medium-weight materials such as voile, gingham, chambray, and sheers of silks and synthetics (fig. 77).

1. Turn under the top of the hem about ¼ inch.

2. Machine-stitch about ¹⁄₁₆ inch from the fold. If the hem is straight, use about 12 to 15 stitches per inch. If it is curved, use 6 to 8 stitches to the inch and pull up the underneath thread to ease the fullness in top of the hem to fit the dress. Lay out on a flat surface to keep the hem flat against the garment.

3. Pin or baste, about ¼ inch below the fold.

4. Slip-stitch the underneath side of the hem to the dress, along the stitching. Take back stitches every third or fourth stitch. This method keeps the stitching under the hem; it gets little abrasion from wear or laundering; and the stitches do not catch and break. It is a quicker method than hemming along the fold and gives a neater appearance on the right side.

Flat hem, slip-stitched.—For heavier fabrics—linens, coatings, spun rayons, failles, and similar fabrics (fig. 78).

1. Pink, overcast, or machine-zigzag the edge of the evened-off hem.

2. Machine-stitch about ³⁄₁₆ inch down from the edge. Pull up the underneath threads, if necessary, to ease in any fullness.

3. Slip-stitch, rolling the top edge of the hem away from the dress; catch the stitches into the row of machine-stitching.

Machine-hemmed.—One of the quickest ways of putting in a hem is to use a machine attachment or a swing-needle machine. The hem is particularly strong for school and utility clothes.

1. Turn under the hem edge ½ inch.

2. Baste the hem to the skirt about ⅜ inch below the folded edge.

3. Fold the skirt back on the basting line and stitch (fig. 79).

Machine-stitched hem.—For aprons, shirts, circular skirts (fig. 80).

1. Machine-stitch around the hem, ⅛ inch from the edge.

2. Machine-stitch around the hem again, the width of the wide edge of the presser foot from the first row; these two rows of machine stitching serve as a guide in turning the hem edge up and under quickly and evenly.

3. Turn under just beyond each row of stitching; press; baste, if needed.

4. Machine-stitch around the top and the bottom of the hem. Stitch from the right side with the presser foot as a guide for best appearance.

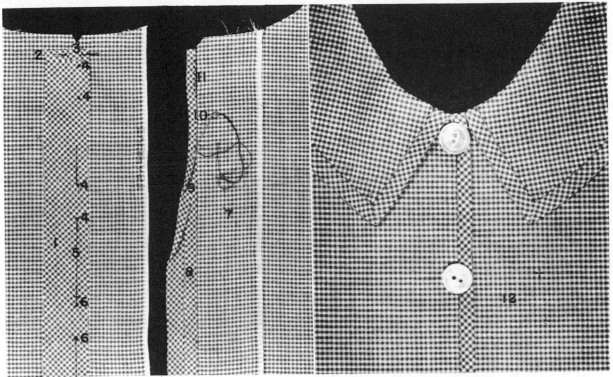

FIGURE 81   FIGURE 82

Fastenings

Strip buttonholes.—Easy-to-make substitutes for lengthwise worked or bound buttonholes on a tailored dress or blouse. To make the finished edge as flat as possible, cut the front facing in one with the front (fig. 81).

1. Cut a strip of straight or bias fabric four times the desired finished width of the buttonhole binding. A finished binding ¼ inch wide gives a neat appearance.

2. Turn under the top edge of the strip ¼ inch.

3. Pin the strip to the garment, with the seam line of the strip exactly over the center front line and the top edge level with the neck seam line.

4. Mark the top and the bottom ends of each buttonhole an equal distance apart.

5. Machine-stitch on the center front line between each buttonhole, being sure to

6. Back-stitch at the beginning and end of each section of stitching.

7. Press the facing to the inside of the garment.

8. Press buttonhole strip away from the blouse.

9. Turn under the outer edge of the strip so the fold meets the stitching line and the folded strip is the desired width. For a narrower binding, trim it down before turning.

10. Overhand the strip to the stitching line between buttonhole openings, taking several back stitches at the beginning and end of each buttonhole.

11. At the buttonhole openings, overhand the loose, folded edges together.

12. Finished buttonhole strip (fig. 82).

Hammered-in snap fasteners.—Fasteners of this type are strong and easy to attach, well suited to utility clothes, but need strong reinforcement to keep them from straining and tearing the garment.

With separate stay (fig. 83)

1. Press the facing back to the right side, turning on the front fold marks. Stitch the neck edge from the fold to the collar point and trim the seam allowance to about ⅛ inch.

2. Lay a strip of firm fabric against the facing, with the edge next to the front fold. Pin or baste in place.

Facing stay (fig. 84)

1. Press the facing to the right side, turning on the front fold marks.

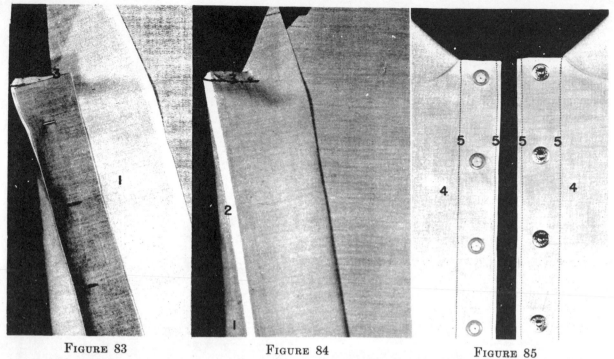

FIGURE 83   FIGURE 84   FIGURE 85

2. Fold the facing back again toward the front, until the straight edge lies along the front fold.

3. Stitch and trim the neck edge; clip to the center front.

To finish both (fig. 85)—

4. Turn the facings to the wrong side; press.

5. Machine-stitch down both sides of the center front so the stitching will catch both edges of the stay. The machine stitching helps reinforce the fastenings. Both left and right fronts should be made the same way.

Adjusting Gathers

Gather by machine to save time and to achieve an evenly distributed fullness. There are several ways of doing it, depending on the amount of fullness wanted.

Ruffler (fig. 93).—A moderate amount of fullness can be gathered or worked into small, close pleats (1) very easily with a ruffler.

Gathering foot (fig. 93).—A slight amount of gathers (2) can be put in quickly with the gathering foot. This foot can also be used for shirring.

Long machine stitch (fig. 94).—When fullness needs to be adjusted to fit, the gathers may be put in by sewing with a long machine stitch, from 6 to 8 to the inch, then pulling up the underneath threads (3). Three rows of gathers—one at the

seam line and a second and a third ⅛ inch on each side of the seam line—help to distribute gathers evenly. This method is an easy way to take care of the extra material in the tops of set-in sleeves (fig. 95) and to work in elbow fullness in long

FIGURE 93

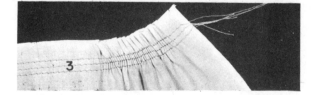

FIGURE 94

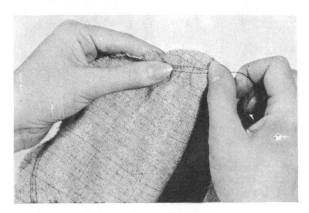

sleeves. It is also a quick but satisfactory way of easing a very full skirt to a small waist. To simplify working on long lengths of fabric, gather between seams, then pull up each section.

When fullness needs to be close fitting, yet adjustable, it can be held in with elastic thread or webbing.

Elastic thread (fig. 96).—Use of elastic thread makes fullness at sleeves and waistlines soft and comfortable. Wind the elastic thread on the bobbin by hand and lengthen the stitch to about 8 or 9 to the inch. The thread gathers as you stitch.

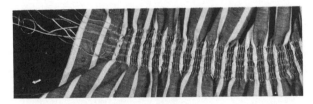

FIGURE 96

Elastic (fig. 97) can be inserted in a casing, or if narrow, sewed on with a zigzag stitch wide enough to cover the elastic.

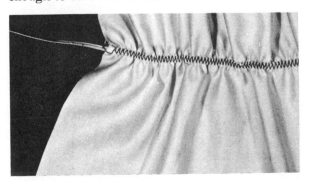

FIGURE 97

Elastic webbing (fig. 98) makes a comfortable, adjustable waistline finish for shorts, briefs, and pajamas. For easy application, divide the waist edge and a snug waist length of webbing into eighths, and pin the elastic to the waistline with the respective points matching. Pin in between these points to hold the elastic in place during sewing. Basting is little or no help here. Stretch the elastic to fit the fabric edge as it is sewed, pulling with both hands to hold it flat against

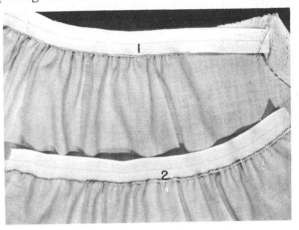

FIGURE 98

the material. Elastic webbing can be sewed on with

1. Straight stitch: Lengthen the stitch to about 8 stitches to the inch.
2. Zigzag stitch: Use the attachment or the swing-needle machine. Adjust to a moderately deep stitch, a little less than $\frac{1}{8}$ inch, so the stitching can stretch with the elastic.

Casing Openings

Casing openings are needed for inserting or fastening a drawstring, ribbon, or elastic as at the neckline, sleeve, or waistline. Two finishes suitable for neck edges and one for waistline openings of pajamas or shorts are shown here.

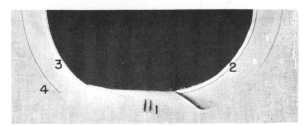

FIGURE 99

Buttonhole (fig. 99).—A neat finish for the right side of a neck edge, sleeve, or waistline.

1. Make two buttonholes by machine, about ¼ inch apart, where the opening is to be. If ribbon is to be used as a drawstring and is to show, make the buttonholes on the garment; if the drawstring is to be concealed, make the buttonholes in the hem or facing. In each case, make buttonholes before the hem or facing is sewed down.

2. Stitch a facing to a curved edge, right sides together, and trim the seam allowance to ¼ inch. If the edge is straight, it may be hemmed.

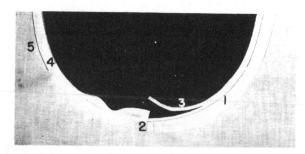

FIGURE 100

3. Turn the hem or facing to the wrong side; press; stitch close to the neck edge.

4. Stitch the other edge of the facing or the hem to the garment.

Hemmed opening (fig. 100).—

1. Shape bias tape to fit the neckline, with the inside edge pressed open, or use a shaped facing.

2. Fold the tape or facing ends back so they just meet to form the opening; pin, baste, and stitch the tape to the garment.

3. Trim the seam allowance to ⅛ inch.

4. Turn to the wrong side; press; stitch close to the edge.

5. Stitch the other edge of the tape or facing to the garment.

In-seam opening (fig. 101).—An easy way to finish a waistline opening when elastic or drawstring is to be used. The opening may be in the side, center-front, or center-back seams.

1. Stitch the seams up to the hem marks.

2. Above the hem marks, press the seams open.

3. Turn under the seam edges to make a ¼-inch hem on each side. If the seams are flat fell, clip the seam as far as the stitching line so the edges will turn back flat.

4. Machine-stitch hems of opening; if flat-fell seams are to be used, stitch one hem and the second row of the seam at one time.

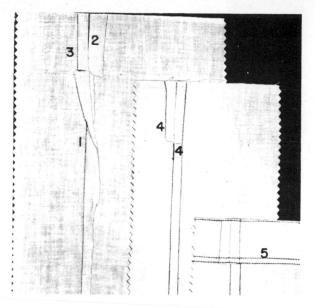

FIGURE 101

5. Turn the top hem to the wrong side. Machine-stitch the hem, making two rows at the bottom and one row along the upper edge. This method keeps the seam opening on the wrong side.

Appendix 2

Clothing Repairs

You may not enjoy repairing clothes, but it does pay off in better appearance and savings for the whole family. Now as always, the stitch-in-time means fewer clothing replacements and more money for other needs.

Using up-to-date methods can help cut the size of your mending pile and extend the life of your family's wardrobe. If family members learn respect for their wearables and something about the high cost of rips and tears, that helps, too!

Although sewing machines and mending aids save time and energy, handwork is an important part of repairing clothes.

In this publication you'll find information on—

- Mending equipment and aids.
- Basic repair stitches and their uses.
- Reinforcement of garments before they are worn.
- Patches and darns.
- Mends for damage commonly found in family clothing.

EQUIPMENT AND AIDS

You are more apt to mend promptly and efficiently if you work in a convenient place with equipment and supplies assembled for action. Strong, diffused light is essential for any kind of sewing.

A basket, box, or large drawer can hold your mending and supplies. In it you can keep scraps of fabric left from making clothes or altering readymades, and usable parts of discarded garments—material for patches, buttons, zippers, and other fastenings.

Look over the list of mending equipment and aids given below. Select those items that will help you with your kind of mending. You may want to add others as you find a need for them or learn to use them.

Here is the list:

Sewing machine. Reverse and zigzag stitchings are helpful, but any workable machine can be used.

Iron, pressboard, press cloths, and sponge for dampening as you press. Pressing is essential for a good start and a good finish on a mend.

Scissors. See that points are sharp for precise clipping and trimming.

Pinking shears. Use to finish the edges of fabrics that do not fray badly.

Magnifying glass. Helps with close work.

Ruler. A transparent ruler, 6 inches long, is convenient to use.

Flexible tape measure. It is economical to buy one of good quality.

Threads. Several kinds of thread belong in your mending basket—
Cotton—for general use in colors that prevail in your family's clothing.
Silk—helpful in mending best dresses, coats, and suits.
Linen—for sewing buttons on coats that get hard wear.
Elastic—useful in restoring the stretch in wristlets and neckbands.

Beeswax. Rub on thread to protect against abrasive wear when you sew by hand.

Buttonhole twist. Rework buttonholes on coats and suits with this sturdy thread.

Pins. Buy dressmaker type. Keep in a pin cushion or suitable container.

Thimble. Use one that fits the big finger comfortably and resists needle punctures.

Needles. Get crewel type (with long eyes) in sizes for fine and heavy work. A blunt or round-end needle (tapestry) is best for mending sweaters.

Needle threader. Saves time and helps prevent eyestrain.

Bodkin. Handy for replacing elastics or tapes in casings.

Embroidery hoops. These hold materials taut for hand or machine mending. Embroidery supply shops stock many shapes and sizes of hoops.

Ripping aids. These can save time only if used carefully. Otherwise, rippers can make more mending necessary.

Small stilletto or thread pick.

Crochet hook. This is useful in pulling snagged yarns to the inside of a garment, for making new belt loops, installing reweave patches, and replacing French tacks that hold lining and coat hems together.

Hooks and eyes. Keep replacements on hand.

Snap fasteners. The sew-on kind are used for dress clothes; the pound-in kind for utility wear.

Buttons. Save the extras to avoid buying a whole set in case one is lost or broken.

Darning cottons and wool yarns. Keep a supply on hand that matches the family's socks and stockings.

Darning egg. Use one if it makes your darning easier. Many women prefer to darn a sock when it is pulled over the left hand.

Tapes. You need several kinds—twill, bias, and straight—for reinforcement and finishing.

Net fabric. This is helpful in repairing lace and as a base for some darns.

Press-on interfacing as backing for machine darns; **iron-on patches** for emergency repairs on play and work clothes or socks.

Pencils. A white chalk pencil and lead pencil are helpful in making guidelines as you repair clothes.

Small pencil sharpener and sandpaper pad. Use them to keep fine points on pencils.

Plastic mending tape. Sometimes this can be used to prolong the life of plastic raincoats or garment bags.

Buy Carefully, Mend Less

One way to help keep repair of clothing at a minimum is to check garments carefully before you buy them. When you shop, follow these suggestions:

● Pick types of garments best suited to your family's needs and to the kind of care these clothes will get.

● Check sizes and fit. Getting just the right fit avoids many strains that cause damaging rips and tears later.

● Study style features and trimmings to see if they will hold up in use. Some, although satisfactory in dress clothes, are not practical in garments for work or play.

● Examine the workmanship of a garment, outside and inside, to make sure it is appropriate and serviceable for the material, style, and cut of garment, as well as for the use and care it will get. Look for flaws.

● Take time to pick the best garment, whether clothes are piled in a stack or hanging from a rack. Don't hurry. All clothes of a kind, or even a size, are not equally good buys. While one choice seems as good as another, clothes are made by individuals, some of whom are more skillful and exacting than others.

BASIC REPAIR STITCHES AND THEIR USES

Even if you do some family mending on the sewing machine, you still need to know the basic hand repair stitches shown here. Handwork is often necessary to prepare the damaged area for the machine work.

With certain of these stitches, you can pull damaged areas into shape before darning or applying a patch, fix places not easily reached by machine, and disguise the seam lines of insets or patches. When a mend needs to be practically invisible, soft, and flexible, nothing takes the place of handwork.

All the stitches shown here are helpful in some kind of mending. There are no hard-and-fast rules for using them. Simply choose and adapt them to the problem at hand; keep in mind that the main idea is to make the mend look as much like the original material as possible. In so doing you greatly extend the usefulness of the damaged garment.

Hemming stitches

The running stitch (fig. 1) is especially good if you need spaced stitches. A whipping or slanted stitch (fig. 2) works best if you want close stitches. Notice that the thread in the running stitch is under the hem fold, but is on top in the whipping stitch. For protection against abrasive wear on skirts and the like, a slip stitch (fig. 3) is

best. Between stitches, the thread runs inside the fold of the hem. Many times it is desirable to machine stitch this fold before hemming (fig. 4).

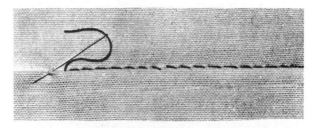

Figure 2

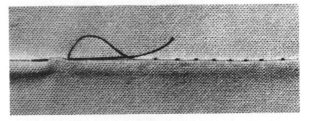

Figure 3

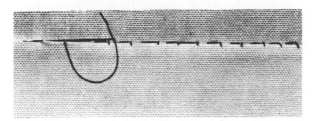

Figure 1

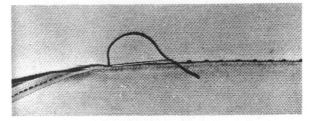

Figure 4

Overcasting (fig. 5) makes a good seam finish to protect cut edges against ordinary, but not excessive, frayage.

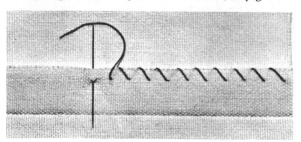

Figure 5

Back stitch

For places hard to reach by machine—underarm seams, gussets, and plackets—the back stitch (fig. 6) gives the appearance of machine stitching. The underneath stitch is twice the length of the top stitch. Top stitching looks like machine stitching because each top stitch meets the next stitch.

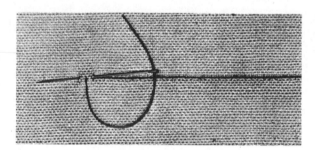

Figure 6

Seed stitch

This variation of the back stitch, in which only tiny stitches show on the right side (fig. 7), is strong, but practically invisible. It can be used to repair zippers put in by hand, and in other places where appearance matters. A long underneath stitch permits a space between small top stitches.

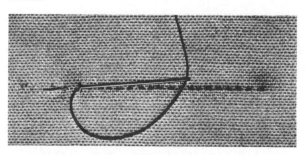

Figure 7

Padding stitch

The padding stitch (fig. 8) is helpful for tacking and holding two layers of fabric in place before machine darning. It also reinforces a darn and protects against inside wear.

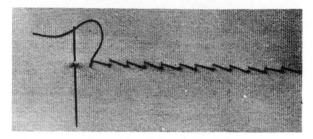

Figure 8

Blanket stitch

The size of the blanket stitch depends on its use. Make it large for edge finishing as in figure 9, very tiny for strengthening weak corners.

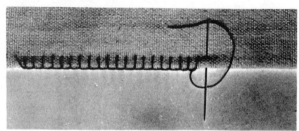

Figure 9

Rantering stitch

This technique is used in disguising unwanted seam lines—and is especially helpful in heavy, thick fabrics where the stitches can be buried. To do the rantering stitch (fig. 10), pinch the seam line between thumb and forefinger and stitch back and forth over it in V direction. Pickup only one yarn on each side of seam line. Pull thread up close.

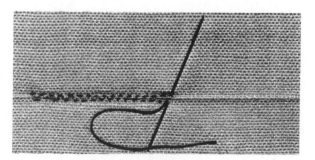

Figure 10

Lacing stitch

This one can be used spaced (fig. 11, *A*) or very close (fig. 11, *B*) for pulling two cut edges together temporarily or permanently. Spaced stitches are often helpful in restoring the shape of a damaged area before darning or applying a reinforcing patch.

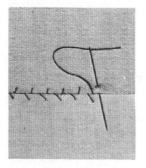

A

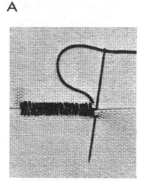

B

Figure 11

Catch stitch

Use it on the underside of a garment to hold the cut edges of one fabric against another. The depth and spacing of the stitch depends on the material and kind of repair. Figure 12 shows how the stitch is made. Labels in coats and suits are often held in place with catch stitch.

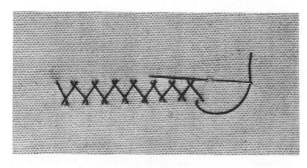

Figure 12

Overhand stitch

If you want to join two folded edges, the overhand stitch (fig. 13) may be used. Take stitches in the very edge of the folds as you hold the two edges together.

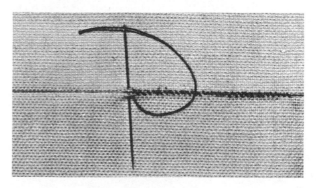

Figure 13

Buttonhole stitch

Often the edge finish of a worn handworked buttonhole can be reworked as shown in figure 14, *A*. The buttonhole stitch can also be used to improve the appearance and prolong the wear of machine buttonholes (fig. 14, *B*).

This is a good stitch for sewing on snaps and hooks and eyes because it gives long wear and an attractive finish.

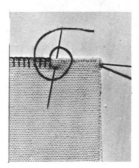

A

B

Figure 14

Before you or a member of your family wears a new garment, check it over. Strengthen any weak spots and correct any manufacturing errors that might cause trouble later. Often there are faults that catch your attention at once; other weaknesses may not be so obvious.

A few well-placed stitches and repairs at this time will help you get the best possible service from your purchases. It will be worthwhile to check the points listed here.

Dangling threads

Fasten off thread wherever stitching ends. Pull these threads to the inside and tie securely. Or if threads are long enough, run them through a needle and fasten with a few stitches—or pull the threads inside a hem or fold.

Stitching

Rip out and restitch any broken, knotty, drawn, or crooked stitching. If this repair is inside a garment, let replacement stitches overlap at each end of the space you have ripped out. If repair is on the outside, pick out enough stitches so you can pull thread ends to the inside and tie them. Replacement stitches on the outside should just meet, not overlap.

If the spot is difficult to stitch by machine, back stitch by hand (p. 3) to replace the machine stitching.

Seams

Seams that are too narrow can sometimes be stitched a little deeper to make them hold. If the material is fraying—but not badly—simple overcasting of the raw edges will make a seam secure. If the material frays readily, it's better to run a row of machine stitching near the cut edges—then overcast (p. 3) or finish with zigzag machine stitching.

A good way to guard against broken stitching when seams are curved or bias is to stitch them again, using a short stitch, about one-sixteenth inch beyond the seam line.

Hems

In readymade dresses, hems are often loosely put in with a stitch that ravels. This kind of hemming is a convenience if the dress length must be changed, but in use it is hazardous.

Stitching that ravels and pulls out can easily result in a sagging hem that tends to catch on shoe heels. Better pull out such stitching and rehem with secure stitches between hem and dress (p. 2). Use silk thread for extra strength.

Bindings

To save a big mending job later, make sure that all bound edges are securely stitched. If binding is sewed too close to the edge, rip the binding open, ease the binding in a little deeper, then restitch.

Stretchy edges

If the outer edges of necklines, collars, plackets, armholes, and pockets are cut on a curve or a slight bias—rather than on the straight of the goods—they sometimes stretch, then tear.

To prevent such stretching and tearing, stay the outer edges on the underside with straight (twill) or bias tape. Or rip open the facing, and sew tape next to the edge, then restitch facing.

Vents, V- and U-necklines

Narrow twill tape laid next to the seam lines or folds, crossed at the corners, and firmly stitched will strengthen these openings without adding bulk.

Belt loops

In readymade clothes the ends of belt loops are simply pulled to the inside and knotted. These knots frequently come untied and pull out. To fix them, draw the loose end to the inside of the dress with the help of a crochet hook. There the loops should, if possible, be securely attached to a side seam with a few strong stitches.

Pocket corners

Before strain on pockets tears a garment, reinforce the pockets at the corners. For a pocket on a blouse, a sloping bar of stitching, as shown in figure 15, may be enough.

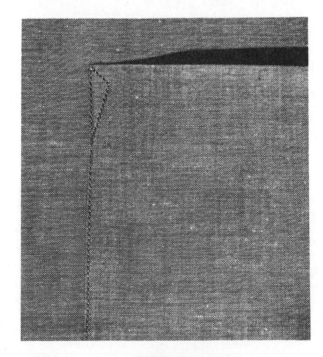

Figure 15

Skirt pockets need more protection. On a gored skirt, lay a piece of tape on the underside in line with the pocket top and stitch it in at the corners (inner stitching), and, if possible, extend the tape to nearby seams as shown in figure 16.

Plackets

Plackets of all kinds get considerable strain in wear and ironing. Extra stitches and tape across the ends on the underside may prevent serious damage.

For a placket that is merely hemmed and tapers to nothing at the end, reinforce with a small pleat and bar tack as shown in figure 18, *A* (before) and figure 18, *B* (after).

Figure 16

A

In a flared or circular skirt, reinforce pocket corners with a tape supported at the waistline (fig. 17).

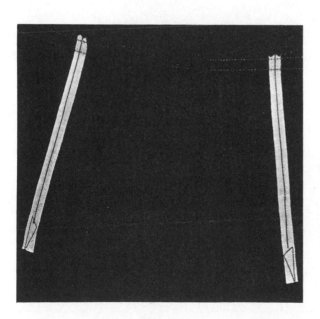

Figure 17

B

Figure 18

A thread tack at the turn of a continuous placket eases strain that in time damages a garment (fig. 19). The tack does not show when the sleeve is buttoned.

Pointers on Patching

• When a damaged garment is a bit shrunken and faded, patch it, whenever possible, with similarly shrunken and faded material. This helps hide the mend.

• If new fabric must be used to patch a washed and shrunken garment, shrink the patch piece. Otherwise, the finished patch may not lie flat after laundering.

• On a readymade garment, patch material can usually be taken from a facing, hem, pocket, or sash.

• If fabric has a design, slide patch material beneath the hole until the pattern matches. In a fabric like corduroy that has an up-and-down pile, match the direction of the pile. Careful matching helps disguise a patch.

• Cut a patch with the grain of the goods, making sure that lengthwise and crosswise yarns match those in the material you are repairing.

Figure 19

PATCHES AND PATCHING

Hemmed Patch

This sturdy patch, made by hand, is appropriately used on most washable fabrics, including cotton dresses, blouses, and some work clothes.

To make a hemmed patch, follow these steps:

• Mark smallest possible square or rectangle that will remove damaged area.

• Cut along lengthwise and crosswise yarns.

• Clip each corner of the hole diagonally about one-fourth inch deep (fig. 28, *A*).

• Turn under slightly beyond ends of these clips. Crease sharply or press. Take care not to stretch the material if you crease instead of press.

• Slide patch under hole until pattern matches. Pin in place, then cut patch about one inch larger than the hole on all four sides.

• Baste patch in place. On outside, hem with fine running hem stitches (p. 2 and fig. 28, *A*). Stitch closely at the corners. Let stitches catch in very edge of the opening.

• Turn edges of patch under about one-fourth inch on the inside of garments made of lightweight and washable materials. Snip out bulk. Baste and hem invisibly (p. 2) to garment (fig. 28, *B*). In thick materials, catch stitch (p. 4) edges of patch to garment or pink edges of patch, and seed stitch (p. 3) in place. Choose the stitch that best suits your material, but make stitching as inconspicuous as possible on the right side.

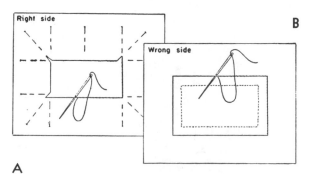

Figure 28

Inset Patch

If you want a durable patch that is almost invisible, the inset patch is a good choice. It is suitable, however, only on firmly woven materials where the patch can be matched to design. Inset may be put in by hand or machine stitching.

Here are specific directions for making an inset patch:

● Cut out damaged place on grain of goods to form rectangle or square as required.

● Clip corners diagonally—about one-fourth inch deep. Turn edges under just a little beyond the ends of clips and with grain of goods. Press.

● Match patch piece to hole and pin or baste to hold patch in place.

● With white silk thread, slip stitch (p. 2) folded edges of the hole to patch piece, catching very edge of folds with stitches about one-half inch apart. Then slip stitch at each corner.

● Turn garment inside out. Stitch patch in by hand with overhand stitches (fig. 29, *A*) or stitch by machine, following the fold lines and the white thread of slip stitches. (For overhand stitch, see p. 4.) Begin machine stitching midway on one side, stop at each corner; with needle down in fabric raise presser foot, turn, and continue around the patch. Then remove white thread.

In clothes that receive light wear, the seams of this patch may be pressed open to be less noticeable. Overcast edges to prevent fraying (fig. 29, *B*). (For overcast stitch, see p. 3.) In utility clothes in which service is important, press seam edges toward the garment, then top stitch on right side. This holds seam edges flat inside the garment.

In thick fabrics—corduroy or heavy suiting—cut the patch piece just to fit the hole. Back it with a piece of lightweight press-on interfacing fabric that is about one-half inch longer on all sides of the opening; then machine stitch back and forth over the cut edges and, in the case of corduroy, between the ribs.

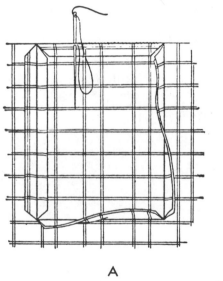

A

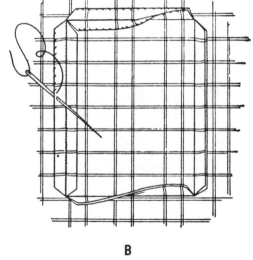

B

Figure 29

Straddle Patch

You'll find the straddle patch an excellent patch for repairing damage at the base of vents, continuous plackets, and slashed, V, or square necklines. Watch such places and apply this patch as soon as signs of strain appear.

Here is the way to make a straddle patch:

● Dart any tear that may have occurred and finish edges securely.

● Cut a square patch, not necessarily of the same material as the garment unless some of the outer fabric is missing. A plain fabric is better if the garment has a pattern or is thin. A 2-inch square is usually adequate, unless damage is extensive.

● Turn and crease the four sides of patch.

● Remove binding from placket point.

● Close the placket. On the inside of the garment, center this patch astride the end of the placket. Because the patch is set on biaswise, it will give and not tear.

● Machine or hand hem patch in place on its four sides.

● Slash patch to placket end and restitch binding in place. Figure 30, *A* shows finished patch on wrong side; and figure 30, *B*, patch on right side.

If this patch is used on a square or V-shape neckline, a section of the straddle patch will have to be removed for smooth fit.

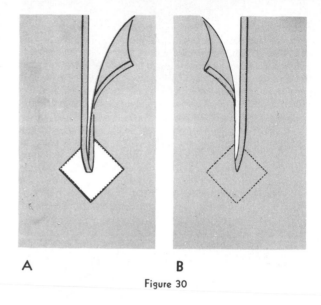

A   B

Figure 30

DARNS AND DARNING

Tips on Darning

● Study the weave of the original fabric, and reproduce it in your darn as closely as possible.

● Work under the best light available.

● Use a fine needle and short thread. Long thread pulled back and forth across a torn place, or a worn hole, may pull and stretch damaged area out of shape.

● Darn on the right side of material, and blend the darn inconspicuously into fabric around hole.

● Work for flatness. If yarns are pulled tight, the finished darn puckers and looks drawn. Too loose stitching gives a darn a puffy look.

● Draw mending yarn or thread through yarns in the cloth itself, rather than in and out of the material, whenever you can. Take small stitches. Be especially careful not to draw the thread taut when you make a turn. Run the stitching unevenly into the cloth surrounding darn. This prevents a hard and heavy line around darn.

● Pull ends of darning yarns to underside of garment and cut off, but not too closely. Work in such a way that all raw edges of a hole or tear are on the underside.

● Steam press finished darn from wrong side. If material is wool or napped, brush darn to lift nap.

Plain Hand Darn

A plain weave hand darn is the best way to mend small moth-eaten or burned holes, and most other small holes. Large holes are better repaired with a patch.

Here are guides in making a plain hand darn:

● Snip away ragged edges of holes.

● Choose darning yarn or thread that matches the fabric closely in color, weight, and luster. Too heavy yarn strains the surrounding fabric and makes the darn noticeable. Mercerized cotton thread usually blends into fabric around a hole better than yarns from original fabric.

● Work back and forth, lengthwise, across the hole and far enough into the fabric to strengthen the thin or worn area that may surround a hole. If there is no thin area and stitches can be run into the underside of a woven fabric—not pulled through to the outside—the darn will be less noticeable.

● Weave crosswise, over and under the lengthwise yarns, and again into the surrounding fabric (fig. 34).

Figure 34

Pattern Darn

Use the pattern darn to repair small holes in suitings or dress fabrics with distinct weaves.

Before making a pattern darn, study the weave carefully to see how lengthwise and crosswise yarns are interwoven. A magnifying glass will be helpful at this point. As you darn, reproduce this weave as closely as possible, using matched thread or yarns to best suit your fabric (fig. 35).

Figure 35

Machine Darn

A machine darn is a quick way to repair straight, three-corner, or jagged tears, diagonal cuts, and similar damage. Follow this procedure for a neat machine darn:

• Place damaged spot right side up over an ironing board, sleeveboard, or other flat surface. Straighten and trim any tangled and frayed yarns.

• Cut an underlay from lightweight press-on interfacing fabric. Make underlay no larger than necessary to reinforce and hold the cut or torn area in place.

• Slip reinforcing fabric underneath damaged area— adhesive side up. Hold it in place with pins. With yarns combed precisely in place, cover mend with a thin cloth to protect fabric, then press. If necessary, it may be pressed again from the inside.

• Use thread, either silk or fine cotton—whichever best matches the luster of your fabric—in a slightly darker shade than fabric. Machine or handstitch back and forth over the damage, usually with the grain of the fabric.

• Trim away any excess of the reinforcing fabric, unless the surrounding area needs it for strength.

• Then tack reinforcement invisibly to the back of the fabric with padding stitches (p. 3).

• If damage is a three-corner tear, a snag, or badly frayed, machine stitch both crosswise and lengthwise.